A NEW MIND
for Christ

VOLUME 3

DELUXE EDITION

Angelo Melendez

Library of Congress Control Number: 2020923020

PAPERBACK: 978-1-953791-43-6
EBOOK: 978-1-953791-44-3

Ordering Information:

For orders and inquiries, please contact:
1-888-404-1388
www.goldtouchpress.com
book.orders@goldtouchpress.com

Printed in the United States of America

CONTENTS

POEMS AND STORIES

FINAL THOUGHTS

Me without GOD I suffered struggle drugs plus the streets can't believe he brought me this far life's so so deep I'm eternally grateful for life GOD'S what I'm gonna speak don't let the devil take you again to be lost in defeat JESUS CHRIST is for you leave the world follow the truth your nothing without him GOD I'm nothing without you say it with me !!!

John 15:5 (KJV)
5 I am the vine, ye are the branches: He that abideth in me, and I in him, the same bringeth forth much fruit: for without me ye can do nothing.

Angelo Melendez a.k.a veelito

I grew up a troubled teen fighting, doing drugs and selling them I grew up in the Mott Haven section of the Bronx sports and music was big in my life playing sports baseball football and basketball but basketball and music was always a passion an outlet for me I wanted to play ball professionally but school wasn't my thing my first bad decision I dropped out of school so hustling and music was all I had left I did music for the world while I ran around the streets up to no good thank God I survived the streets all glory to God I've been through so much but when I was changed because of Gods mercy things were made clear to me it was when I realized I was living a lie and after the lord turned my head he taught me one of the most important lessons ever which is stop letting the devil lie to you I really could understand that and see that I was living a lie. And that everything I did before I did for Evil I was a destroyer only God can show you what love is and the right path God is the only way and I thought my life was over but God showed me I can do whatever as long as its for him I have a mission through music its just to Glorify God and bring people to him however I can right now but me and my brothers Gio Frankie Shavon and Ronnie have been moving together for 5 years now as a unit God and I'm proud to be a part of the Bronx Holy Flames organization preaching through basketball changing lives and now we also have a clothing line called Anointed by his presence I'm glad to be here and know it's time to give back with the talents that Jesus, our Lord and Savior, gave to me. I have second chance to do the right things in life music for God was always the next step so right now its TEAM S.W.A.T with my brother Eric Mingo A.K.A Christflow forever Team SWAT stands for the Brave Saints.Worriors .Angels. Theologians and the Humble Sinners. Worshippers. Anionted. Testimonies bringing you the Holy spirit through music I'm proud of our entire movement. It means the world to me more than money, more than fun, and more than fame. We are here to encourage, all to come to christ to inspire and create with love & support through music & basketball. Im a walking testimony that probably should have been dead a long time ago but God has me here standing as a different man and Im a firm believer that it's not what you've done, it's what you are doing now all glory to God forever because God changes your life to succeed only God can change poeple only God knows what's right for you so put God first.

CHAPTER 1

My Definition Of True Blood

If getting money is in your blood well you could gather around but since money won't get you christ now's your time to cash out to those lost you can be found I was picked up from the ground if you listen to your spirit you can find that crown it don't matter what you've been through or what you've done only our father and savior knows your true outcome I know your stees get that paper that's all in your ear hustling in the streets watching your rear blood sweat and tears for years just facing your fears hoping one day you in the clear while God is pulling you near but you ain't trying to hear you in the wrong dream what you thought was for you wasn't for me I've been there so I understand the way you bleed there's more to life then what you need there's more to life to believe like how Jesus died for us he bled for you and me. Amen!!!

Times up

He's everything so you could climb his hands are the hands of time but most don't have time for the creator of time so how can you define who's really by your side if you can't spare time so you could shine and the dark occupies your time and your watch says money on my mind so you love the world and waste your time it's such a crime he gives you time so you could fall in line breath so you could find his light that is divine but you say never mind where is the respect you out your mind because he's kind you think your doing fine he gets you through rough times whenever your in a bind and you still walking blind your not inclined but he holds your grand design just something to keep in mind I know what I'm doing with mines I'm chasing God till I die before times up and I'm out of time.

Brothers

Forgive me lord Im only a worm but I am concerned for my brothers that are lost in this world and need to learn that hate only brings hate tell me how it's gonna turn into the love that we need from you lord that we yearn In Jesus name we must of not have learned from abel and Cain your world will never change if your heart remains the same plenty times in the Bible we are told to love our neighbor that it's one of the Bible most repeated commands from the creator I think only a fool kills his enemies and his brothers but a servant of God kills his sins and loves others.

See for yourself

New year new test new life new respect for breath I spent years leading friends to go a stray I was a mess telling them to have another drink another party never rest let's do bad who cares smoke on to relieve stress I guess forgive me but you want forgive yourself if you don't confess the pain will stay forever only God knows best it took me over thirty years to deliver this message now I'm stressing God is real and everyone in this world needs his presence.

Let God change you

Only God can save us only God can shape us only God knows our heart because he made us don't give up please fight don't let the devil rape you he already got you lost soon he's going to break you our choices take us where we are and the devil continues to snake us destruction till death of your life is where he wants to take you meanwhile God still loves you and he awaits us we are nothing without the lord only he can change us.

CHAPTER 2

Pause to discuss drugs

Drugs

Drugs are bad God is good stop the madness get out of darkness let God be your happiness let God be your guide to the life that your supposed to live just let him in.

Although drugs can feel good at first, they can ultimately do a lot of harm to the body and brain. Drinking alcohol, smoking tobacco, doing all illegal drugs, Can all cause serious brain damage to you and destroy the human body. Some adults or teens believe drugs will help them think better, be more popular or do things better all the devils lies. Others are curious and figure one try won't hurt. Others want to fit in due to peer pressure is a big problem watch who your kids hang with.

Many teens use drugs because they're depressed bring your kids to the house of God church where God can work with them or think drugs will help them escape their problems. The truth is, drugs don't solve problems — they simply hide feelings and problems. and problems will remain, or become worse. Drugs can ruin every aspect of a person's life our lord Jesus Christ and savior is the only one who can help you who can heal you change you or fix you.

Here are the super facts on some of the common drugs.

Alcohol

They say you can't have a party without liquor stop drinking and put God first

This liquor can and will destroy your life

Slows you down

affect judgment and coordination. Drinkers may have slurred speech, confusion, depression, short-term memory loss slow reaction times.

Poisoning your life away

Highly Addictive

Alcohol is a depressant, which means it slows the function of the central nervous system. Alcohol actually blocks some of the messages trying to get to the brain loosing brain function. This alters a person's perceptions, alcohol causes greater changes in the brain, resulting in intoxication. People who have overused alcohol may stagger, lose their coordination, and slur their speech a lot of car accidents because of drinkers this is the devil's nectar.

Cocaine and Crack

Both highly addictive both kill your pockets your hopes and dreams gone

The devils drugs affects the central nervous system, feeling unstoppable intense super power and energy. cocaine and crack can stop your heart and you could die

Ecstasy (MDMA)

Teens hit raves girls are usually raped or just get pregnant by the wrong guy

Party it up nothing from the world holds your SALVATION Only GOD

This drug combines a hallucinogenic making you crazy all emotions, both negative and positive, much more intense. You might wake up in jail this dangerous drug will destroy you

Heroin

This drug puts you to sleep taking you the grave and destroying your life completely where you feel pain if you don't have it this is a sad drug.

Marijuana

Popular drug that kills your mind and brain cells and destroys you also keeps you from God a major distraction

Nicotine

We also have crystal meth and molly I aint even gonna get in to those too it's just crazy it's safe to say drugs make you crazy and destroy your life.

Some over the counter drugs are worse then illegal drugs shows you how much certain people care about us as long as they making money nothing will change as long as you don't care about your life nobody does so go ahead keep drinking partying smoking your kids are gonna follow your lead I was blessed with a chance to change I was just like you smoking drinking partying chasing money sinning and now i just chase God only he knows everything for real and what he has for you is amazing trust me matter of fact don't believe me see for yourself because I'm not perfect nobody is only him but thanks to God I can finally see that I'm going the right way all our lifes we just been doing whatever living for the moment but lost in it spinning our wheels following the trends doing whatever to be who people want us to be or think we should be well not me not no more I got him he guides me please I'm not special I understand ya'll I've been there right there right where you at tripping and I still make mistakes because the devil will always try to catch you but God will protects you and now almost everything is a learning lesson for me now and no matter what he's with me it's crazy and i see that arrow I have a light and I know I'm on the right path I swear it's so amazing and exiting cause I don't know where it ends but I know its the right way I know most of you are just going through the motions saying I'm living life but are you really and if you don't know that your going against God you are but here's the kicker the devil don't care about your health or that you could die using drugs Naa his joy comes from the disrespect to God by destroying your temple that's what your doing another great lie by the devil telling you it's okay to drink and do drugs knowing your body is thy temple and it's sacred the master of lies has so many people dis respecting God in so many ways it's not funny so please believe me and think for 1 second there's another way God is real and he loves you what do you got to lose you done tried everything including all drugs now try God he won't fail you.

Stop letting the devil lie to you

We have to be strong not weak aren't you tired of defeat we have to stop letting the devil lie to us his skills are unique he is the father of lies and all he wants to do is destroy us the minute we think this and that is ok it's all slaughter for us allday we turn around now we dumb far away and we are lost far from God but that won't be me I can't let that happen I gonna go hard I won't go back we have to stay awake and look for God put him first thats that read the bible and praise his name stay in church forget the fame the devil will use anyone in his deadly game such a shame he'll destroy you stay sharp God has a plan for you all we have to do is listen to him and continue your mission take the righteous path start living you could be dying but I'm fishing God bless you all its time break the devil and his traditions.

Forward progress

Progress in the process of learning with God as long as you don't give up the lord will back you up you can't lose touch mistakes are lessons true blessings of his presence if your spiritual ears are listening i guarantee you'll get the message once you begin understanding the bible you start understanding people you realize there struggles you know that know one is evil know one really means to be deceitful they just want to be equal stuck in this world upside down please let the bible teach you jesus is gonna show you so please let him lead you.

Without God

You can't do nothing without God but you keep trying hard still doing your own thing while you still chasing the stars he still watching you sending you messages from a far but you so caught up in the world you ignore your own scars faithful servants everywhere messages through your peers you don't care you turn your back you don't want to hear what do we know well we know we all going to die for sure but how and where we going is the real question though are you going be an example from the lord while you here to your family and friends sharing Gods presence with no fear or just empty vessel living your life to regret it and the devil uses you to get across his filthy message who you with make ya mind up homie time don't stand still we fall we all fail and only God keeps it real but I'm keep striving to do what I'm told and no matter the obstacles I'm still on that heavenly road keeping Jesus Christ close make sure everybody knows but the real question goes to you where will you go. Amen!!!

Love each other

If you have love you can't hate lives matter your trust is great you live happy you understand God is pulling you by the hand you sacrifice for others you love and help your brothers and never disrespect your mother and if you suffer you never blame others just pray for your troubles Gods plans nobody knows but the love he shows grows till it expose those dark souls that bright light will switch a foe to a friend if you ain't got love that's not him without christ that's your end let me tell em again you choose you see the news but Gods life you misuse or refuse authority and power you abuse or lost without a clue in the streets confused you busy following what everybody do but here's a little truth jesus loves you and if God loves you then the love starts with you.

Just waiting for the call

Maybe we met mabye didint but our love is written I love your spirit and voice is so uplifting we know what we want we live for God your my rib and I see heaven in your eyes I love you and you love me and we both worship God he is in our relationship if he wasn't we'd fall apart I can kiss you forever our love is so intense for you and God I go hard and thats who we are we most happy in his presence our love is written in the stars but we are always exited when we do great work for God your prayers keep me going and our belief keeps us strong we belong together no one understands us but us and God makes us who we are he fills us daily when we touch and we put him first you complete me and I'm here to heal your scars me you and God are the meaning of true success we catch each other if and when we fall and love each other more every step we are spiritually connected with God we are pure no one can break us apart our hearts combined is a true force you and God is what I talk we are eachother crutches when we walk your the best everyday we are together our love can't rest we acomplished so much together your God's blessing girl and Im blessed our love will never fade we passed every test God brought us together in marriage and we are glad we said yes we hold each other's hearts our love burns away our flesh I need you I want you thank you lord you know best and lord knows I love you together we will go far I think I know who you are I'm just waiting for the call.

CHAPTER 3

Pause to humble yourselves

You ain't gotta be a drug dealer you ain't gotta be a gangster you ain't gotta be a thief pulling guns ain't the answer there's another way in God we put our trust and faith we pray b4 every thing and we pray b4 we play.

Life is about learning you grow and learn the sins and sinners of this world want you to burn only God is the answer the teacher the king you made this far let God show you more thing's.

You've Listened before, but hear me now

Do you know him ? If you really do you would do the right things and nobody could tell you to follow no other kings because you know he is real and your heart and spirit no the deal don't let no one tell you to let Christ in your heart for the thrill or friendship let's chill or just follow God for blessing cause if you don't believe then backsliding is the lesson so if you're invited to church please go for the right reasons go cause you believe not cause someone that your pleasing pick up that bible start reading God's words you gonna fear it because real recognized real yup when they hear it so when God speaks to your heart through someone it's gonna shake ya spirit you'll know it's real 100 percent now you gonna live it until then don't front for no one on top of any podium please I did this for a long time i was So Gone in the past I went to church just cause they invited me and i probably heard some real stuff but went back blasphemies I was addicted money power respect was my casualties lord forgive me for my sins and ya'll haven't heard the last of me.

You have a chance to let God lead you before its to late.

When I was younger I wanted to be a ballplayer but I let the streets influence me into dealing and using please don't make this mistake put God in your life and he will show what's important I'm blessed still to be able to be involved with basketball so my message is follow your dreams with God driving the wheel I wish I could go back I wasn't half bad but I can't so don't waste your time and your God giving talents on nonsense pray b4 you play.

Lord God forgive us all for our sins we stumble we fall but we get up to my fellow christians keep fighting we know we need God daily we can't do anything without you i pray for everyone to understand that nothing in darkness can live in the light that's why many choose to stay in the darkness but today God wants you to step into the light so the darkness can't overtake you we love you lord because you are light the light that's separated from the darkness the light that shines our path through the darkness our father our lord and savior Jesus Christ the light the Gate to salvation you are the only way in Jesus name I pray God bless us all in the name of the Father the Son and the Holy Spirit. Amen!!!

Still there still here

He still there even when you don't care even when you giving up when things are rough he protects you from the devils touch God's love is for life but you call him when you need him take a blessing then you leave him and his words you don't believe em but I'ma praise him and keep em plus I got prayers for you that you wake up like I did one day and speak the truth cause you headed to the lake of fire unless you surrender to the messiah you thinking I'm just living but your bieng fooled by a liar father of lies got you living real comfortable right so you feel you don't need christ man your so unwise unlike me defriend me but I'ma talk christ till I'm empty or till God come and get me till God come and get me.

Ladies lost

ladies don't let vanity destroy you i got something for you it's ok to be beautiful but dont let it control you you're most beautiful when you praise God and your loyal and use the beauty inside you thats why God called you use what God gave you instead of letting the effect of popularity enslave you and you wonder why they play you you acting just like they do let the lord guide your spirit he'll show you the real truth only God can shed the light to show you the real you.

Dead Fishing

Keep thinking you good go ahead keep thinking you know keep thinking life's a show without God you won't grow quit believing in man keep deceiving yourself keep praising wealth you could be loosing ya health just look at how many fell unaware of your surroundings sleep walking street talking dead walking outlined in chalk fam you destined for more can I get witness catch me fishing see this posted on the book but will you really listen you don't get it you not seeing I'm different you don't believe em so I spit the holy spirit cuase his words I'ma keep em yup Jesus Christ I'm breathing his word is what I'm eating while your lifes bieng mistreated possessed by these demons but I'm here screaming with my fishing rod leaning let God bring you life I'm dead Fishing this evening. Real talk

CHAPTER 4

E 4/Chase GOD

Same one that never missed a party breaking night in streets living them hood rules trying to avoid beef I had to chase paper had to stay lit swearing I'm the man believed my life the shh It's me yes shall we proceed i was dealer and a sinner a destroyer from the streets chased money chased girls chased coke chased weed the one that was always drunk crazy life indeed i was so lost now i gotta new boss he broke me out of prison now I'm a prisoner for the lord yes of course that's from ephesians 4 learn from Paul take the blinders off transform that old man is gone and a new man is born huh lost before for so long I believed wrong funny how I swore I was on running from the source running from the cross in through one ear out the other time to floss sure i know where you at but from God you so far real real recognized real let me tell you who your are a servant for God yea this christian got bars but I don't need applause because it's a gift from the lord to speak hard for his cause to Pierce through your heart understand christ died for you so homie play your part let christ change your heart and mind because it's his design he put me right here at this hour at this time to change your life of crime so God can bring you life you sinning all the time and Now I'm telling you what's right my brother you was made to shine by his grace and his might God the real truth Chase Jesus Christ the light aaite !!! (Chase God)

It's not you

We got tons of work to do for God I'm hoping that you hear me you ain't gonna be shopping or sitting around looking pretty silly me silly you for thinking that you could just get me for the type of relationship I need your not ready it's not that your inferior you just don't fit the criteria I need a prayer warrior with God in her interior so i could really fight back I'm sorry but it's like that I need a princess from God thats a true champ not a blood sucking vamp or a chick with a dim lamp I'm flattered but no thanks you a broken tank can't help me in this holy war I already know who you are I'm there for you I care for you I'll pray for you thats all.

God be with you

You dont like me no worries he already told me you pulling away slowly cause christ is my only you don't know me cause i refuse to hang around fonies cause I smoke heaven and drink scriptures and spit testimonies If I left you sower this year forgive me this hour but the power of lord is moving through me getting louder for starters i hope to proceed to plant seeds until you see that God is the one you gotta believe so you could branch out of your tree to be whatever he want you to be till everything is flee yeah a new year with new ears for you hear and hopefully his word will become clear before you leave here dont let his glory past by you try him before he trial you im praying till God shine on you hope that light find you and put three types on you father Son and the holy spirit uplift life on you homie i you wish christ on you.

Shopping At The Fall

I'm still waiting for you to realize the life you lead is no surprise you chasing endless world supplies while christ cries through your children's eyes how could lead them to destruction vanity is your function till you meet the lord naked and recognize your corruption stop the assumptions I'm a repented sinner with jesus a broken man was fixed before your eyes believe this a crowd around your frown makes you a clown so you smile for the town blend in but you down if you don't feel like this now soon you'll hit your wow and J gonna break you down and show you his crown break the chains that surround because your mind is bound when he moves off that cloud that's when you'll be found but then he will lift you up with a heart beat for your sound so go ahead doubt em get mad when I talk about em but all you need in life you'll never have without em his fruits you can't buy so keep eating spinach thinking you popeye but your kids could be finished you need to trust God plus his love has no limits God bless in the name of the Father the Son and the Holy Spirit. Amen!!!

Wake up

It's time to wake up they played you ever since you came through you've been surrounded with evil told to do what they do pushed away from the truth they told you God ain't cool unless you have what they have in other words don't be you its a set up teaching division and hating multiplication corruption destruction

till kill us or keep us in the matrix and make sure we don't say
shh they even got you loving the same sex disrespecting God im
vexed but they will regret they been trying to stop his blood like
playtext but im covered in it wrapped up leather avirex time to
hear his name flex jesus forever raigns yes he's the only one that
came and went over and over again you know my king the last
one standing when we play chess he controls death while you
waste breath watch what you say next your not saved yet ya
like the elephant never forgive cuase ya don't forget but I got
a little mouse called faith he going make retract your steps be
correct for God's benefit respect and fight your flesh and huge
change that's obvious you gotta past a big test gotta go through
the process only way to be blessed you focused on everything
else but God's the beginning and the end stop the nonsense.

CHAPTER 5

Pause and ask yourselves these questions

Please ask yourself these questions if your a non believer ask yourself these 2 questions

1. Do you want eternal life or eternal death . 2) Do you really want to know your God.

And If your a Christian ask yourself these questions

1. Are you trying to do what's right or are you intentionally disrespecting God.
2. Do you think your doing enough for the Kingdom of God.

LG

Please decide to live for God my life is for God (LifeGod)

How could you continue to live a false life that definitely ain't real you hear and see God's work but you still spinning your wheels another lie from devil so you continue to chill in a life without christ wow how empty you feel you wanna change and you really feeling strange and but the fame you get for your sins feels amazing you get cheered on for smoking you get cheered on for drinking cheered on for fighting for twerking for living this crazy life you live that supposed to lit it's just a trick leading to hell a disease that got you sick dis obeying God's laws cause you popping you think killing what God has for you and what he's done for you how far could you sink lost in the blink of and eye the devils lies are a trip I was there swore I was winning just corrupting my gifts destroyed plenty people around me and thought I was the Ish until God showed me my mirror and I couldn't resist recognized for your kids they gonna follow your flick the movie you live and all of that crap that you do and you spit I see mommy loves money mommy loves chilling daddy got girls he's always with other women well I'm following the word of God thats how I'm living you need to break out of prison and make God your decision sword tucked under my arm man I gotta go hard I hope you see how God sees and my life is God.

Look @ me please

Look at me I want to be noticed im not joking please i need your focus please tell me that I'm important self love will destroy your moment and all the time you spend for yourselves is hopeless but look at me I'm skilled I'm unique check my pedigree my body is awesome sexy served up like a recipe eye brows on fleek everybody wanna be next to me its about my talents my looks and my energy ya need to get off mines nobody is stopping me I love the attention I forgot that God died for me you really don't care what you ruin your like tell me how I look please tell me how I'm doing I gotta be first to me second place is lousy so if I here them talking I wanted to be about me yes check my dress peep my make up i got this what I'ma wear today please look at my outfit I'm bout this life huh so childish nothing but the devils logic stealing glory but God is the real promise we all need to stop this ya caught up in the nonsense the world that we live in was jesus christ conquest he the one that died so that you can accomplish so for everything that you are he's thee accomplice it really ain't about you look how these selfish stars get me I'm just a servant of God that's what I'm is please it's not about me just know that God lives for years I was lost and heartless walking around in the dark so godless no amount of money could change hearts and spirits God is no gimmick his words are written and living in this christian the air that he gave you you waste it on your vision what appeals to you don't appeal to the lord that's risen but your lost in your flesh you want the glory that's giving I pray for you now please change up your traditions God's watching and talking but you don't want to listen if you cant give God the glory then good riddance !!!

Lost chance

I know i know i know i got it under control I'm going through somethings this is temporary yo i promise im gonna change ima do better i promise i wont let up i promise im gonna get up im gonna go back to church soon just give some room I will forgive her don't worry I know what to do let me live my life I'm gonna be alright i just need a break I'm struggling everyday is fight I feel you i hear you i know what you mean huh look leaving his side ain't the answer i know you blowing off steam I know you took a hard hit I know it's hard to stay clean but don't put up screen on your understanding you can't lean you need God in between please let him set your scene comeback to christ repent before your last chance please could be a nightmare or a dream just trust God and believe he's calling you don't leave he's the answer that you need just drop down to your knees but you keep putting him last and like this you won't advance so i pray you make it back and don't end up a lost chance.

The Armor

This aint about titles your sword is your Bible the lord is your survival but you gotta let him guide you listen peep it his word is lifes secret he will protect you and correct you but only if reading and seeking he's your healer your protector your true love connection your breakthrough he made you through him so he could take you hold you and mold you into the glory your supposed to be something special giving fruit like he told you but the world takes your emotions and switches your promotion then the lord gotta go get you from deep down in the ocean your like a pearl in his hand sliding off because you can how many times he's gonna go and pull your head out of the sand you need the lord like please take me but your life is on maybe your lukewarm running into traffic screaming God save me yup thats crazy spent know time with him lately but if your in Jam your gonna call on him daily a disrespectful man and lady lost like a baby told to stay put but went off away from safety how God gonna fight for you if you won't let him guide you through preaching but not living everything you want others to do so keep your guard up stay close to the father otherwise your just shooting yourself with no armor.

Fake love

God created you raised you to be something special but what did you do disobeyed thought for you when ahead and ate the fruit came through died for you and his persecutors he forgave them too you got no clue you selfish true you really ain't got no excuse for the things you do that fake love gets deeper only visiting God on easter no pastor no preacher wont submit won't get cleaned up lack of commitment not submitting to the law and scriptures that are written disobedience to the one that's risen continue living however tripping and got the nerves to ask God what you getting you deserve Nathan my hearts breakin no time for God cause you money making or in the club girl booty shaking but I bet you gonna tell me I'm hating or that I got scared and thats the reason I'm changing whos really faking it's you life to lead but worst if you know the word cause it's blasphemy because your bieng dis loyal perpeisly not hurting me knowing your supposed to only serve G.o.d with that fake love you just a disrespectful tree unable to give fruit well thats what i see if you lost ima pray cause I'm worried for you but if God give you to the devil then I feel sorry for you so if you know him and dont show him for you truly I'm scared but if your a non believer I pray he touch you get prepared the time is right now this moment right here surrender to the one true God yup oh yeah something needs to happen follow christ so you can change but if you don't take action things will be same and your the blame. Amen!!!

CHAPTER 6

Stay on the path

Ask yourself these questions daily

1. Does God know you ?
2. Do you live for Christ ?
3. The things you do are they for God's name and glory or are they for you in God's name and Glory ?

I'm Hurt for you

Hurt cause when i fall I fall close to where God can lift me but when you fall your moving closer to the enemies entry because you don't really believe because your lost in your dreams your still living for yourself I'm trying to live for G.o.d and I really can't do nothing if you refuse understand since you refuse to comprehend the world today are the devils hands guiding misleading telling you bad is good broad is the road that leadeth to temptation understood and no matter what I say no matter what I do its all up to you but your still gonna do you because you believe in you but you need to believe in God because life is so hard plus your blinded by your scars thinking your the boss thinking your in charge and you won't submit so God can really Change your heart we can't do it without him but you believe that are but you really falling apart you tripping cause your in the dark you living with the worst of you thinking that your shining through confused chasing views chasing money chasing dudes just keeping up with whoever or whatever they telling you running while God is calling you nobody could tell you truth plus you don't wanna lose and for everything theres an excuse your a know it all and you know where you going true this use to be me this probably a bunch of you this is why I cry and pray this is why I'm hurt for you.

Following my creator

Nothing but Trends and traditions a bunch of street suggestions the world telling you what to do who to follow what's the news what to get who to check just chasing money and sex you don't see the disrespect not following the lords request the word is alive the verb the action the one and only thats christ he died for your sins but the world is telling you what's right God's the light of the world you in the darkness without em your creator knows what's best but everyday you just doubt em chasing the world full throttle for worldly possessions got you hollow you know evils guiding the world so tell me why would you follow get in your word God gonna show you you ain't from this world and I aint leaving christ for nothing not money or know girl this challenge ain't simple but God will help you get through choose God not the world cause Jesus really loves you so God is my function check my fruit don't make assumptions and remember broad is the path that leads to destruction.

ANGELO MELENDEZ

Choose wisely

I didn't see before but I see now the regulation a broken generation lost in translation young girls bieng misguided by the world's domination changing communication let me tell you what you facing they got ya disrespecting for money or penetration how you figure he love you but got you committing fornication then if he play you you'll take em back with no hesitation praying he'll change but that dont happen in every situation he might forever be the wrong choice ain't no explanation cheap thrills sensation till you reach a bad destination together for the wrong reasons battling complications and if God ain't with ya you'll end up in damnation your the creators creation but won't follow his illustrations just cause he gave you children good sex or gifts to you thats love don't know what grace is to me its time wasted and the world call it dating ya gotta love God to love eachother this connection aint basic put God first face it its a spiritual love Foundation with christ that ya chasing that relationships amazing cause God's in the middle they'll be no altercations and evertime you look up God with ya still communicating listen he probably cheat on you he probably beat on you mistreat and defeat you but you still lean on em you need a man to teach your kids the word of God and vice versa not to teach em to sag his pants run the streets and throw curse words up violence death murder selling drugs to be a earner chilling on some corner he probably be a burglar getting lit just to turn up carrying all types of burners living life nervous cause ya aint teach em God's scriptures and verses ya the worst quit the worst is she blinded by lustful urges and she ain't trying to hear God she still trying to make it work kid but no God so there's no love in him it might be worthless and some girls don't wanna be alone but God looks beyond the surface but there's pain in your heart and you left in the dark and want someone to protect you so you stay where you are but God siad come find me he'll guide you like he guides me and place you up highly you ain't gotta live with Mr. Grimy theres true love for you just wait on God's timing then choose the right man girl you gotta choose wisely.

Being Cool

I gotta be cool cause they watching gotta be cooler then them so if they take a step I'm taking 4 to pass them i love the public to love me my people's got my back be im focused on this shmoney I'm living cuase I got me I'ma push it to the limit counting digits they gonna feel it when I pull up I'ma crush it outfit gonna be so siick its cool to hit it and quit it its cool to do some stealing its cool to deliver a beating its cool we just chillin but whatever they do ima do better or faster even though I didint know i was disrespecting my master created in God's image not other way around so without God homie your soul will never be found created to praise and follow christ and be an example of what's right but we impressing eachother in the dark meanwhile God is the light the devils lies bring devils night salvation ain't in the world salvation is in the word salvation is in the verb salvation is God ya heard cause the world is absurd so kick the devil to the curb so disrespecting the laws are cool in his book but I ain't trying to get written down with evil living with crooks the book of life is with christ keys to heaven and hell nice so forget the street life for approval to get recognize I don't care what they do I ain't gonna follow the hype on a highway to hell smiling thinking you alright you desperately seeking applause i know walking away it's hard I know walking away is tough being cool got you behind bars feeling you living large this coolness is taking you far thinking you a star you don't even know who you are so you could be cool all you want you just hiding your own scars I know the truth you ain't cool you ain't nothing without GOD !!!

We don't know nothing at all

All day every day we think we know what's best we make the wrong choices we suffer with regrets I know the word I understand yea you standing under your mess you refuse to hear the message but you wanna make a request I believe in God word homie thats a nice tale they dont know you in heaven don't even know you in hell stop embarrassing yourself you can't lie to God how many got healed and left and forgot about the lord we the only ones that dont listen to the word of God written the whole earth obeys God but not us we different we got our own plans we got our own agendas busy following the world trying to be the next big pretender run our mouths against everything and don't listen to anything truth in our face but we think we moving towards our destiny plenty Ls definitely moving with the enemy till we left for dead on a road but we still no better we say I learned my lesson but that ain't true at all cause after we on our feet we run back into the same wall so drop to your knees pray to God repent and learn real talk I'm concerned I dont want you to burn stumbling in the dark can't find your way you stuck but refuse to flick that switch like I'll find it hold up thinking you in control gambling with your soul only Jesus knows it all we don't know nothing at all.

CHAPTER 7

Tears of shame

I was doing what everybody else does I had no love ran the streets sold drugs as my shoulders shrugs I was convinced life was rough so I had be tough I gotta survive I gotta take over gotta stay live continue to strive money is my drive living unwise wasted years chasing all empty things outside theres a never ending supply of nonsense you could buy things that fill up eyes but leave you empty inside all things that keep you from seeing the passion of christ not knowing life is a gamble you just rolling the dice but you getting it in and the party life gonna keep you hype chasing d evils and you ain't even knowing your flight destination to destruction but your pockets aaite your shorty look tight plus you popping bottles tonight dont even know whos your enemy but you got a gun or a knife in a spiritual fight with no God no tools no light not knowing that your a miracle creation of life I feel I've wasted God's time and I thought I was right so now I cry and repent to God with all my might God's life God's will be done breaking chains despite whatever path you in I pray you bump heads with christ I think ya better recognize before you meet your demise don't want you waking up surprised burning in the lake of fire oh yeah I care depart from sin everywhere give your life to christ let the darkness disappear lord forgive me and my peers I disrespected you for years I just didn't want to hear chasing girls money and gear drugs had me living unclear so I repent nothing but tears but your mercy got me here your grace keeps me near your presence makes me cheer and you took away my fear so I gotta let you steer and wait for you to appear you're everything I didn't know I needed way before I changed forgive my display I'm Unworthy with tears of shame.

It's about God

First off God created you not other way around ain't no way lyrics can tell the composer to change the sound I'm lifted gifted only by his grace in my place my story is for his glory I race at his pace plus he created this road so I'm moving his way all glory to God forever updated my resume so worship God stay strong and don't worry about what's wrong God gonna have mercy on who choose to have mercy on and if he end my song to glorify his throne then I appreciate my life I was truly blessed to be born romans got me going I'm hype peep the fruit of my loins allday you chasing shackles I'm chasing spiritual coins so eat up enjoy food for thought today hoy T.B.E is God not pretty boy Floyd hope these words will grasp you I love you and I have to tell them it's about God not about the amount of money you have dude and I'm only half way through hope the scriptures don't pass you he died for me so I live for him and I'm glad to put christ first had to get at you weather God save me from furnace or not ain't bowing to that statue that's your loss chief obedience got me free the old me died with christ now he lives in you and me so get to praising worship our God he's amazing the only one to defeat death with much love thats so patient but you run around hating disobeying following satan its your life its your way but your sadly mistaken while he was preaching evil was contemplating Stephen got to see the glory of God before he was taken while bieng stoned to death to me that's breathtaking it's all for God's glory so I'm patiently waiting put your faith in God everybody needs saving he blew breath in your lungs after he was done creating there's no need for applause please just follow God's laws it ain't about us homie it's about God.

No Colorlines

Our lord and savior Jesus Christ is life yes God is my purpose and I'm a witness a servant a unworthy failure that was chosen outspoken to tell you fight your flesh the fight Club is open put your faith in God not in man I'm not joking me included stay secluded depart from sin what you loosing your blinded the root of evil got you snoozing no excuses is it sorcery, jezabel or drugs aint that today's music what's your amusement or that fake prophet that's just cunfusing lord excuse em forgive em the mind is still in prison using the word of God to create more hate and racism God's great start worshipping believe that God's risen because he brings the promise with em from his throne where he's sitting I ain't kidding you better listen God's for whoever believes in em and whoever fulfills his laws and God's mission I choose submission to the lord from now till the end of time Jesus Christ loves us all and he has no colorlines.

CHAPTER 1

Comfortable with sin

God created you but your cultivating sin to other witnesses can't see the differences Jesus died for you but you won't live for him can't see the prison you in how sad you live for your sicknesses you spend more time drinking smoking partying brings such distances from the king within stuck in the darkness believe your life good you grin then when Easter come that's the only time you visit him such wickedness but without your creator you cannot win start listening fearing the Lord is knowledge you need to fight your skin your flesh is weak we need Jesus daily believe I love you and care for your salvation so I plant seeds but heaven won't come from me or no man indeed God's not dead put your faith in Christ let him lead but instead you chasing greed living selfish for your needs rejecting the most high ignoring the prince of peace and he still reaching for you even though he already bled for you and me but you busy with the world making sure your life flea your worldly possessions lead to hell without God you cant breath how far will the enemy take you how long before you bleed if the blind is leading the blind what do you expect to see we where created to bare fruit but you chopping down trees even Sampson beat his chest and thought wrong stop thinking that strength is yours when your strength comes from the lord above you won't notice when the holy spirit is gone repent and give glory to God because everything for his cause for sure so respect his laws and forget about applause that fame got you lost tell me what you deserve if he bled on the cross this life is not about you listen God is everything but you walk around selfish you comfortable with sin.

Don't get it twisted

Some use God's words as a defender some read and believe what they want and misuse it for their agenda some wanna create wealth and don't want to surrender doing what others do just differently our God we play with em some use the word for slavery some use it for racism I see you create your own God for your freedom you could do whatever you want as long as you believe in em saying lord forgive me but I'm Keeping my sins with me you got it twisted you created a God for your sickness God's laws don't change but you wanna play the victim saying God understands but your fooling yourself trying to trick em trying to make your own restrictions and make sense of your own decisions so before it all goes down repent or you gonna miss em he's our savior our deliverer he'll have mercy on who he choose because we Gotta follow God he aint gotta follow you his law is not to be bended conformed to our liking we have been warned listen close before the thunder comes the lighting you wanna know what's really frightening we are driven by our own excitement my God my way like you the only one fighting selfish ain't it the truth I'm sorry if this love hurts you but the glory belongs to God and you still living to exalt you talking like my God this my God that he gives me help like if God is only for you and not for nobody else humble yourself follow the lord daily keep your connection this world is full of evil don't catch the next infection stay grounded do what's right for the lord cause he's life and you have to not for people or for fame or worldly things that attract you let Christ be your guide and don't get distracted from your mission apart from God we are nothing so don't get it twisted.

Truth talk

I never believed I would be speaking this way my life views from strange days my thought process changed more brave since being saved from tragedy I could see life actually a new uplifted personality walking perfect in Christ's is a reality I understand your trips as you walk on the 3rd rail I didn't believe too well either my conscience was in a cell the darkness will keep you comfortable on the road to hell plus the confusion thrown around will leave you shocked in shell there's a why in God's hands your life will magnify he'll use you as a instrument for other souls to survive so alive getting wise I want God to be glorified the holy spirit makes me cry when I fail he makes me rise and the pain I feel inside cause you wont give God a try you missing out on this high only with God I fly he the reason you got by but the devil told you lie God's the truth I can't denied stay connected like Wi-Fi don't wanna be in short supply when the enemy reach my side I don't want you to burn the devil is out to destroy kill and steal if you never heard it like this God's 100 percent real open your eyes and be smart God has a plan for your heart a new life so play your part this truth talk for your walk. Amen!!!

Temporary life

I'm good I got this what to wear what to buy I'm making my own rules I gotta get by I gotta get high I got money I'ma survive

I'ma definitely be alright where the party at tonight its ok to have a good time homie I'm on my grind or they say I don't drink liquor all I do is drink wine God knows that I try but I barely got time for him but he wants me to be happy and shine you out your mine do you really no the lord or are you following evil you gotta follow God's laws so that God will keep you but you comfortable in the darkness because you living for the world you put your money phone sinful pleasures first even your girl that God never gave you because fornication ya'll a slave to all you doing is following the world we'll see where it takes you if you love God you chase em your life is praise and worship you can't stop talking about the truth Jesus Christ keep you working you know you need em daily he's the only one that's perfect and you would rather spend time with God because he's worth it he's the vine he's eternal he's more then anything you can purchase but you listening to the devil lies giving into sinful urges vanity all is vanity this world is such a tragedy nothing could ever fill me the love of God carries me my life belongs to God money won't save me its sad to see all those dying confused and lost ever so rapidly damage seeds living for worldly things that are not permanent but I'm full of God's encouragement so forever I'll be serving em full of the holy spirit Grateful to be one of God's chosen men living my life for Christ trying to stop you from burning fam so recognize God matters And let him hold your hand recognize God matters he Got the only plan recognize God matters only with Christ you can do the will of God he holds your salvation hope you understand he's the truth repent because were nothing without Christ where's your soul gonna go are you ready to sacrifice am I going to hell or heaven am I truly living right God is the only thing that matters in this temporary life.

ANGELO MELENDEZ

Short Glory

No matter what group or gender what race or religion if this world was left to one race there will still be killing if this world was only blue aliens they still be chasing fame money killing insane drugs what a shame the truth is we been lost our way God bless America yea right really man they forgot his name dear lord Jesus Christ is life please make a change put God in your life this wickedness is just pain ya look and sound dumb rest in peace Muhammad Ali a great Muslim we hate Muslims we love gays wake up and start looking such mislead fools no wisdom no tools just following the news who's next to persecute but at the end we all lose cause God is for everyone even you but we abandoned our lord and savior we ain't following his rules homie wake up if you got a son teach your shorty put God in your story we all fall short of God's glory.

CHAPTER 2

I choose him

Lord forgive me for my sins I repent once again this word is as much for me as it is as much for them and I want them to know in there mind spirit and soul that you are real and in control I'm just a servant playing my role we have to repent constantly and speak honestly and tell em Jesus Christ is the gate we need Christ everyday just believe and have faith because God's the only way.

It's your choice to chase money things of the world in that nature it's your choice not to believe and not to follow our creator even worst if you believe and your purposely going against your maker oh how quickly your mislead by fools and devils and God's haters hope you don't think you going to heaven just cause your baptized in Christ fella God weights our actions daily your testimony is forever its your choice even if we're chosen to drink the devil's poison to listen to the devils voices and making his choices 2 equally evil people either way choosing the worst fam he got you wasting time corrupting your mind believing in the father lies party party party just continuing to destroy your shine its your choice not knowing if there's 70 or more rapist in your section to go outside naked expecting to learn a lesson it's your choice to pull your pants up to curse people out as a your

Answer you smoking different things but you really don't want cancer it's your choice not to prevail it's your choice just to fail you chose to be a criminal but you don't want to be in a cell you knew the consequences but you chose to be in jail free will let's you choose what story they gonna tell but you already made your choice you choosing to go to hell your choice your life you the one that abandoned Christ plus he knows your choice you chose already I hope you chose right some are walking around sentenced for judgment from our lord some got there one way tickets because they avoided God's call play with the darkness if you want the word said depart from evil and sin it's your choice what you do for me I choose him.

Prove it

Lord forgive me for my sins I repent once again this word is as much for me as it is as much for them and I want them to know in there mind spirit and soul that you are real and in control I'm just a servant playing my role we have to repent constantly and speak honestly there's no doubt in me lets tell em Jesus Christ is the gate God is love not hate they need to believe and have faith because God's the only way stand firm in his word and never turn away All that God does for us and all that he's done meanwhile we disobey all day and only call on him when we want that fake love we thought was enough we so unpure we need God daily to show us and we need to love him more he deserves more then what we can give him God's real I ain't kidding we can't only talk Christ we gotta live em check yourself daily to see what you doing can't follow the world and it's nuisance if you love God prove it.

Weak flesh

Lord forgive me for my sins I repent once again this word is as much for me as it is as much for them and I want them to know in there mind spirit and soul that you are real and in control I'm just a servant playing my role we have to repent constantly and speak honestly passionately wait on the lord so we could see what he's got for our tree move with God make sure to tell em Jesus Christ is the gate they need to believe and have faith because God's the only way.

It's ok we don't expect you to get it in one shot this process is the toughest plus you unconscious raised in nonsense conformed to there ways since the beginning of your days I'm embarrassed to say such pain I've caused along the way (please forgive me) its not a game temptation threatening your elevation taking steps towards Christ then something tries to kill your motivation we need God daily they wanna see me caught up or turned to a lady but the love I got for God got my path on safety it's still crazy I feel you the way that you've been talking lately that was me living shady from bottom God came and changed me I was there it's easy to do the devils work and not care it's hard to follow God's laws homie for this you not prepared I quadruple triple dare you to come to this side yea I was a coward scared to run with the truth but now I'm not scared only of God's wrath because of him I'm going last stop following the world fam come on take off your mask God's the truth and the truth is G.O.D the spirit is willing but you know the flesh is weak.

Our Father's day

Lord forgive me for my sins I repent once again this word is as much for me as it is as much for them and I want them to know in there mind spirit and soul that you are real and in control I'm just a servant playing my role we have to repent constantly and speak honestly there's no doubt in me lets tell em Jesus Christ is the gate God is love not hate they need to believe and have faith because God's the only way I give all Glory to God always happy Father's day.

Happy Father's day to all the fathers and step father's nobody is perfect some father's do the hurting some of us don't deserve kids some fathers are not worth it but some are still learning but all father's need God and some are hardworking and some do really love and have great concern some are really talking from experience and just want there kids to learn I didn't listened to my father and he died before I could start I know now that he was right now that God changed my heart I'm sorry dad for not listening or giving you a chance to teach you told me life will be heavy but I laughed and bounced to smoke weed but now I see after my life was failing in the streets and I've realized all this time I've been weak but before my defeat I met the true father I need and now I can preach what God has done for me and the world needs to believe that he died for you and me so find your true father yes God is our creator his arms or open with love do it now not later I'm grateful for my life I love all my kids and my neighbors but I'm in love with my father Jesus Christ our lord and savior !!!

Dangerous grounds

Lord forgive me for my sins I repent once again this word is as much for me as it is as much for them and I want them to know in there mind spirit and soul that you are real and in control I'm just a servant playing my role we have to repent constantly and speak honestly and tell em Jesus Christ is the gate they need to believe and have faith love your brother like yourself chase God and not wealth put God first and you'll never be last loosing your spirit as well.

Now really watch what you say telling people there saved that's why they go back to the world and continue to live crazed just cause they accepted Christ that don't mean that there great and only God will be God you gotta pass away from the dust you came you leaving the same way temptation is always on his way from God's hands don't stray you must sacrifice for God and live for him everyday just cause you accept Christ don't mean you leaving with him you gotta follow his laws for life and really live em if you love em that's what you'll do because it's not about you it's about everybody bending there knees to God's truth the Gospel of Christ Jesus who restores those in pieces keeps you from going off the deep end the bread of life that I'm reading he defeated death on the cross the resurrection we believe in the only one I'm seeking that's who I'm feeling the only one that can take away any type of diseases with healing there's evil in the world much blasphemy is on the rise such a crime stay wise don't let corruption change your mind keep you ear to lord inclined they ruined God's designs everyday it's so troubling they disrespect him they spit on his covenant but entertainment you loving it accepting it makes you a part of it though we're challenged by temptation don't give into the devil's nation rebuke and stand firm in word keep praising don't be fooled by mockers fake pastors fake doctrines stay guided by the holy spirit avoid false prophets you got this stay connected keep your faith get corrected by the word that's injected depart from evil in your section keep Christ as your protection stay humble with respect kid the lord is perfection so stay in his presence in confession he's a miracle a walking blessing preaching mercy grace teaching lessons can't be higher then the most high what you smoking you'll be rejected God is omnipresent and your destined to be in heaven but the devils lies got you threatened I know I was once bitten the devils taking plenty with him but I say only if you listen let God be your decision roll with Christians on a mission and stay close to the father yup that should be your roster cause no weapon formed against you shall prosper follow the one true crown it ain't about being down a fool is a clown no need to look around fear of the Lord is wisdom soon that trumpet gonna sound our lord is profound and we need Jesus in our town Switzerland's creating portals man we on dangerous grounds.

CHAPTER 3

Ungrateful

Lord forgive me for my sins I repent once again this word is as much for me as it is as much for them and I want them to know in there mind spirit and soul that you are real and in control I'm just a servant playing my role we have to repent constantly and speak honestly passionately wait on the lord so we could see what he's got for our tree move with God make sure to tell em Jesus Christ is the gate they need to believe and have faith because God's the only way.

Some got baptized and left did a little bit of God work then dipped they quit then wonder why they Got issues in there mist they lost there grip they flipped lost there true gift there relationship with God there so ungrateful it really makes me sick plus there's a list of people that stole spiritual things there fean's but they have only hurt themselves they have destroyed there own dreams some came to Christ for a blessing crying for a healing and after God healed them they back in the streets screaming some came for a girl they got her then left Christ in a situation like that somebody gotta pay the price leaving God is never alright especially if you no the word how you accept get baptized then bounce that's absurd you claim you knew Christ if you did where you at back in the world again dodging the devils traps it was real when you needed Christ but after that you fronted you forgot about the lord once you got what you wanted you should honor God by serving him for you on the cross he hung thank you for everything you've given me and I know there's more to come I've come this far I'm stunned want forget where you bring me from and I will appreciate your gifts living for Christ with the world I'm done I'll never leave the truth fam you must of never had em if you have em you gonna chase em till the end until you grab em no matter whoever hate you you'll never let them take you from God nobody will break you stay connected willing and able Jesus will never forsake you he will lift you because he made you but I'ma tell you what the problem is that most of us are ungrateful.

Where you taking me & Where am I going)

Lord forgive me for my sins I repent once again this word is as much for me as it is as much for them and I want them to know in there mind spirit and soul that you are real and in control I'm just a servant playing my role we have to repent constantly and speak honestly passionately wait on the lord so we could see what he's got for our tree move with God make sure to tell em Jesus Christ is the gate they need to believe and have faith because God's the only way.

They say your my friend till the end I'm down for you down for me its all funny let's party do drugs chase money we just living life old or young either way they say I'm doing great yes the world can relate it's taking you astray you dressed in the times looking good up to date might be on your grind up in school or out of state think you totally fine but the world run your mind my flesh is a crime and you around me bagging dimes both ways curses out your mouth all day while I'm busy trying to worship the lord and continue to pray and keep the lord with me such a hassle lord bang your gavel I won't be rattled rebuke evil skedaddle everyday a battle you hate often dodging coffins might forgive and don't forget ya mind haunted maybe you flaunted got beef constant but you think your honest don't see ya problems you going full throttle I know there won't be a tomorrow If I get caught sleepy hollow where I'm going if I ever leave God and just follow eternal sorrow the word is my life you need to sacrifice with all your might I pray you see the light get wise stop and think what's your life your fruit tells me how you living day and night where I'm going if I aint got God where you taking me if you ain't got Christ.

If you knew him

Lord forgive me for my sins I repent once again this word is as much for me as it is as much for them and I want them to know in there mind spirit and soul that you are real and in control I'm just a servant playing my role we have to repent constantly and speak honestly passionately wait on the lord so we could see what he's got for our tree move with God make sure to tell em Jesus Christ is the gate they need to believe and have faith because God's the only way

If you new him everything gets dropped Just running towards God your stomach in knots just giving him props you never could stop you would feel the pain when he's disrespected you would want all you friends to get corrected and to stay connected you would give up whatever for his lessons and his presence you would speak with conviction a powerful message and pray that it spreads to the world so infectious oh yes bless the day since my awakening I appreciate grace from our king there ain't nobody or nothing better then the lord of all things and that's why I sing for better or worse it's glory to God for life in every aspect of your world you try to put him first right you pray daily and you not confused and sin bothers you and you repent constantly and you see how the lord was abused for you pray for those that are hopeless you appreciate his closeness guided by the holy spirit so you see all evil motives your chosen so your focus is everyday put your hope in him depart from sin when you start to live for Christ that's when your life begins God is amazing you don't know what you missing his grace his assurance his protection he's the reason that I'm living so I beg for his forgiveness for you and for me lets all worship the lord if you new him you would agree don't put your trust in anything we need G.o.d if you love him you live for God if you new him you would believe.

Don't be fooled

Lord forgive me for my sins I repent once again this word is as much for me as it is as much for them and I want them to know in there mind spirit and soul that you are real and in control I'm just a servant playing my role we have to repent constantly and speak honestly love all properly wait on the lord so we could see what he's got for our tree move with God make sure to tell em Jesus Christ is the gate they need to believe and have faith because God's the only way.

Quiet as kept they got us jumping from one foot to the next fight the gays hate the church & Muslims such disrespect black Lives matter now hate the cops let's make a mess let's create a war so we can have martial law applause I won't be clapping they got ya fooled for sure and you could do whatever you want but I know God's the cure Many trials and tribulations such a dangerous world turns when the darkness has the wheel when your life is a concern probably heard the wicked will burn but you ain't got the armor most are wicked themselves so they make things harder all karma put ya guards up with Christ he's the one to find an eye for and eye at the end leaves the world blind more brothers left in the dark while God is the light that shines the wicked against the wicked will get em every time if you a killer then you ain't got Christ in your life the prince of peace protects his children plus he got wrath for those who don't act right there's always a trick you mad hype but you gotta know how to fight repent to lord and pray to God day and night word to wise its no surprised our fight is not against the flesh hear my cry it's against the evils of this world that been on the rise since we left the lord hanging then right after he forgave us he died for all our sins but we still hate our neighbors we are nothing but haters now we're mad cause evil enslaved us such hypocrisy from traitors now bow down to your creator Jesus loves us for real and did nothing but show us love repent to the lord and trust he'll protect you from above let the lord live inside you if you search him he will find you keep Christ in your life he's real let me remind you violence just brings violence don't play with the devils rules I pray for all humanity please don't be fooled.

Steal your Joy

Lord forgive me for my sins I repent once again this word is as much for me as it is as much for them and I want them to know in there mind spirit and soul that you are real and in control I'm just a servant playing my role we have to repent constantly and speak honestly passionately wait on the lord so we could see what he's got for our tree move with God make sure to tell em Jesus Christ is the gate they need to believe and have faith because God's the only way.

Nothing more nothing less but stress to damage your talk poison to ruin your walk he got your flesh incredible hulk keep your distance be slow to anger remember Christ is your mission don't let the devil's lies move your spirit out position causing division if you listen I'm going stay in submission in high spirits with the lord yes the one that's risen if you let the devil hype you gonna end up in prison I won't allow it to happen to me you gotta make a decision anger causes destruction corruption you won't be able to function he'll take you to the dark quick he got you making assumptions let peace dwell in your soul let God just take control the devil is out to destroy you but God will keep you whole he's outstanding understand em stay firm with God that's who I'ma stand with won't get caught in anger throw and break the commandments the devil will tell you your right but your reaction will be wrong so close to the promise land and now it's just gone believe me the devil's tricks will have you like a toy oh boy please don't let the devil Steal your Joy.

CHAPTER 4

lol

Lord forgive me for my sins I repent once again this word is as much for me as it is as much for them and I want them to know in there mind spirit and soul that you are real and in control I'm just a servant playing my role we have to repent constantly and speak honestly passionately wait on the lord so we could see what he's got for our tree move with God make sure to tell em Jesus Christ is the gate they need to believe and have faith because God's the only way.

Ignore the interruptions we need God to function the world's rules about love are all wrong leading to corruption no matter how many kids no matter how many gifts he only loves your body so the next chick won't miss he got you convinced I know ma I did the same but once that fake love fade you guaranteed to get played all day her spirit goes with God her body go to the ground love her spirit not the flesh big homie you just a clown ya better shape up you taught her to love money now you hate her lies of love told by many destination break up my heart is heavy wait up you don't even love your self wake up God the creator not Tyler love your neighbor I know love from my maker sweet love Anita baker real love wont touch you without rings that mean forever real love is taught by Christ yup nobody do it better can't fornicate and fabricate that your relationship is great when it's based on sex and drugs oh yes I can relate listen the love of the world is love of the flesh only that's why you gotta hit first fam ya so phony but when God get in the picture he show you a love richer a spiritual connection that grows bigger that only God can trigger your in love with her spirit ya both see God's vision ya both had God before ya hooked up to be one for God's mission Christ her inspiration and yours ya speak Victory and the kids grow up to see true love cause she's your 1st ministry I'm talking true destiny with God in our hearts and what he brings together nobody can ever part you out ya mind love is beautiful love is kind love is patient love will shine love conquers all forever for real in due time watch me grind real love is taught by God you better slow up and grow up let the holy spirit control ya wipe the dirt off your shoulder stay focused dodge them cobras live life like you supposed that don't listen to the devils lies of love that he told ya for sure I need a princess true to God so for real not one taking me to hell listening to the devils Lies of love lol.

Live for Christ

Lord forgive me for my sins I repent once again this word is as much for me as it is as much for them and I want them to know in there mind spirit and soul that you are real and in control I'm just a servant playing my role we have to repent constantly and speak honestly passionately wait on the lord so we could see what he's got for our tree move with God make sure to tell em Jesus Christ is the gate they need to believe and have faith because God's the only way.

Can't stop reading the real can't let the devil steal our children ya dozed off loosing and death is the conclusion I don't find it amusing so lost in this storm I'm praying to stay strong lord change us we're so gone so wrong I'm chasing Jesus Christ not Pokémon it's on but we listen more to evil then God on the throne the message is so clear you ain't picking up the phone I promise whatever have you aint worth the book of Mathew the world is your dream and nightmare unclean the devil got you a jersey are you joining his team keep following I'ma lean towards Luke 14 no what I mean it will cost us everything to follow our king no in-betweens when God come back to conquer and stomp out the monster I hope you on the right side with the right armor make peace with our father and burn your bridges Grab your cross leave the riches enter submission plead to God for forgiveness hope he take away our sickness his word is so precise leave everything for Christ ain't no other way homie I'm talking sacrifice don't let the devil take you the world can't save you not your neighbor not your friends not your family they unable the world is disabled salvation is God's table and you can't get a plate unless your faiths up to date I'ma wait for Lord I'ma pray to our lord I'ma live my life for Christ let my savior pull my cord and I'ma speak about God we must surrender all everything is his yup nothing is yours yes our voice is his heartbeat our blood is his name check our life is his breath our prayers or his steps next I won't quit never the type my encounter keeps me right how God changed my life so I live my life for Christ.

I won't allow it

Lord forgive me for my sins I repent once again this word is as much for me as it is as much for them and I want them to know in there mind spirit and soul that you are real and in control

I'm just a servant playing my role we have to repent constantly and speak honestly passionately wait on the lord so we could see what he's got for our tree move with God make sure to tell em Jesus Christ is the gate they need to believe and have faith because God's the only way.

I know you aint dumb I know you know where I come from since day one the devil been tugging for my soul was full of hate son I spoke evil taught evil lived illegal followed people drugs almost destroyed me glad I never used that needle while moving kilos don't let him beat you how the devil mistreats you man you can't win your life is tainted you cant be comfortable in your own skin living in sin loose the grin because I'm not with it that paycheck that you cash is leaving a damaged spirit chasing gimmicks from the world when you only need Christ in it stop letting the devil lie to you today that's finished fight for your salvation wake up you need to quit it stop following the world when you know it's forbidden the word is already written I'm not kidding forget the fame jack Christian I claim that time for payback I rebuke the devil and all his works in Jesus name this that fix your frame chat where cain at are you against your brother where your faith at Goliath is coming you gone run for cover I'm on my knees for others he'll give you back everything you lost suffer like job suffered get full of the holy spirit blood of Jesus got you covered you need change be strong think about tomorrow you already know God's not dead you just refuse to follow drowning in your sorrow everything the devil gave you is borrowed a golden egg life till that serpent come through to swallow I spit tradition this ain't fiction let your heart listen there's proof that Christ died and there's proof that he was risen and if you let your spirit peak Christ will release you from prison my fishing rod trying to reach you homie make a decision for real I stand on my faith like a mountain God is my fountain lounging holy spirit surround me and the armors the outfit and the more I read the word I feel doubtless God's the promise the devil is a coward I'm just being honest homie silence the violence God wouldn't leave you for nothing forget the nonsense put you finger through his wound so you could believe Thomas I don't wont you lost for being about shhh I got this please don't allow it because I won't allow it.

Just Cause

Lord forgive me for my sins I repent once again this word is as much for me as it is as much for them and I want them to know in there mind spirit and soul that you are real and in control I'm just a servant playing my role we have to repent constantly and speak honestly passionately wait on the lord so we could see what he's got for our tree move with God make sure to tell em Jesus Christ is the gate they need to believe and have faith because God's the only way.

Just cause your great I need to have faith Just cause I'm awake I'll praise you everyday you showed me true love and now its difficult to hate your the reason I'm breathing so forever I'll wait ya to thirsty I promise God did enough for you and me all your talking about presents and wishes but God's not a genie you praying for yourself that's selfish need to learn a lesson when the last time ya heard them say Jesus without talking blessings he will give you a house and a car and money that's horrendous but his bloodshed was expensive I'm good with the resurrection grace and mercy through Christ let's promote him till we breathless my occupation is endless love Christ it's recommended he knows all your desires forgive us lord it's offensive plenty done missed the message all I see this begging fake Christians like to stunt and you ain't put God high once telling God I'll serve you if you give me what I want keep waiting and I'ma talk that talk keep hating I don't work for none of ya my life's about Christ's in the making so give God all the glory cause this world got nothing for me you even took a class and they told us it's his story lol God first praise God forever read the word and believe in Christ trust there's no one better I ain't got no more to tell ya he sacrificed for you and yours all Glory to God you need to love him Just Cause.

Keep Going

Lord forgive me for my sins I repent once again this word is as much for me as it is as much for them and I want them to know in there mind spirit and soul that you are real and in control I'm just a servant playing my role we have to repent constantly and speak honestly passionately wait on the lord so we could see what he's got for our tree move with God make sure to tell em Jesus Christ is the gate they need to believe and have faith because God's the only way.

It's frustrating all I see is fighting and hating the world is disrespecting the lord and most following satan and some debating oh yeah some willingly some unaware some unprepared they perish cause lack knowledge I'm preaching because I'ma share Christ cause I care forgive me but I must walk discreetly if he sees me so who you fronting for you dodging the doctor living uneasy while I hope Christ keep me while I praise em cause he teach me I need him he don't need me your bible screaming read me that paper got you greedy please lord lead me let go let and let God please turn off your TV he will guide you cause he could lead the life he provide you dwelling inside you if you denied him he'll deny you no matter what challenge tribulation or aggravation or what you facing Christ gives what you can handle just keep communication God be our motivation lead us to our destination the world trying to change us surrounded by haters Christ is the greatest lord please take us no way they gonna break us dodging them fakers mostly entertainers they outrageous Jesus stay loving him even when you struggling stay on point with Christ and don't give up wanting em stay under his covenant stay under his covering carry your cross go through all your long-suffering stand firm with God forever ca ca ca come again he went through worst remember his sacrifice when you feel alone or hurt remember you live for Christ and he knows your true worth December will come and go and friends might let you go and death might take its toll but one thing you need to know is Christ he's eternal don't let the devil burn you Christ the reason I'm growing trust God and Keep Going.

CHAPTER 5

The answer

Lord forgive me for my sins I repent once again this word is as much for me as it is as much for them and I want them to know in there mind spirit and soul that you are real and in control I'm just a servant playing my role we have to repent constantly and speak honestly passionately wait on the lord so we could see what he's got for our tree move with God make sure to tell em Jesus Christ is the gate they need to believe and have faith because God's the only way.

No matter what you think is a problem no matter whatever condition let the lord be your medicine make God your decision he hears you he understands just take his hand his words will keep you firm his love will help you stand wake up the devils lies Got you miserable you crying looking pitiful while he laughing because your sinning too getting ridiculed chopped and screwed headed his way he's glad that you played he got you in water circling a drain till you fade away 1 master Christ is my pastor holy spirit will be your answer keep you away from disaster then lead you through the next chapter keep reading before and after God is forever Christ is the alpha omega gonna show you what's better let me tell ya you can't never ever come close to the pain from our dad he was dragged stabbed and bashed while everybody just laughed a huge sacrifice was made for filthy rags we don't deserve nothing be happy for whatever you have lord forgive me I repent once again for all my sins I'm nothing without you were nothing without him follow God for life even though this world is a cancer I'ma slave to one master only Jesus Christ is the answer.

Remain calm

Lord forgive me for my sins I repent once again this word is as much for me as it is as much for them and I want them to know in there mind spirit and soul that you are real and in control I'm just a servant playing my role we have to repent constantly and speak honestly passionately wait on the lord so we could see what he's got for our tree move with God make sure to tell em Jesus Christ is the gate they need to believe and have faith because God's the only way.

Find Christ you searching for answers in all the wrong places most or often angry you could see it in there faces most like to point out what other Christians do but won't take up there cross and follow Christ like they're supposed to pain turns into anger depression kills you faster I praise the one true pastor Christ is my joy and laughter ya toughness is a disaster God knows what you can be is it pride or the devils deeds such tricks always deceive what you put out you receive we need to practice what we preach what a lesson to teach get left under the street for following it pressure by your peers is dominant you not deciding fam steady searching where the dollar went these words acknowledge me corner suggestions misdirection that your minds still impressed with got you jumping the gun catching bullets to your chest fam I'ma follow God's rules don't need to be famous or cool unless its for praising his Holy name I'm one of God's tools you blinded by the world's preaching disregarding the lords teachings when push came to shove you locked up behind bars let Christ avenge your scars I'm walking with the lord I'm talking strength no weakness he will fight for you remain calm.

Stop playing

Lord forgive me for my sins I repent once again this word is as much for me as it is as much for them and I want them to know in there mind spirit and soul that you are real and in control I'm just a servant playing my role we have to repent constantly and speak honestly passionately wait on the lord so we could see what he's got for our tree move with God make sure to tell em Jesus Christ is the gate they need to believe and have faith because God's the only way.

We let the world tell us what's important we waste time on gimmicks some only speak God when misfortune is resin you got a lot of problems but never when you sinning never when you partying smoking and drinking then you front to get your way you gonna play the victim I'm listening you got issues but you won't fix em nonsense always promoted till you end up in prison blinded you against everything he gave you keep letting the devil play you who else better to guide you but the God that made you he who has a ear let him hear about the truth God's giving pick up the bible understand don't just listen read what's written living a life without light lead by darkness in the night while Christ gives you another day to get it right how precise is his love for you while you turn your back ignore truth you point out the rest instead of following like you supposed to do take a step towards God open your heart say yes the lord will recompense the lord will give strength unto his people the lord will bless I suggest confess repent read up pray up stay up time to pick a lane I'm tired of hearing I believe but you serve him however which way which means not really today your fruit tells all you could only serve one master I hate to see you fall you postponing your own blessings this is so uncool the lord plans to prosper you and not harm you God's real trust me please I was just like you running the streets living wicked until the lord came through I promise praise the Lord God up stop delaying Christ is patiently waiting you need to stop playing.

Go through it

Lord forgive me for my sins I repent once again this word is as much for me as it is as much for them and I want them to know in there mind spirit and soul that you are real and in control I'm just a servant playing my role we have to repent constantly and speak honestly passionately wait on the lord so we could see what he's got for our tree move with God make sure to tell em Jesus Christ is the gate they need to believe and have faith because God's the only way.

You still following they taking but I'm chain breaking they say it's just Halloween I say it evil celebration we stand for our faith we are attacked daily we walk in his grace even though they still hating its not us it's what we stand for but I'ma glorify God more through Christ my life has purpose to stand tall most are asleep and won't believe what he came for I pray for all cause I know a blind man saw when I didn't keep fighting and if you ain't got em better get em cause you need that spot light from Christ I'm trying to tell em they gonna do what they won't with you without

God's protection you a sitting duck without God in your section so make the correction I'm here cause of God I surrender it don't matter another lesson I'm use to feeling the tension we could be talking about whatever then my beliefs get mentioned only God is perfection seek and you'll find redemption but instead you wanna talk without perception without conception walking with the devils convention cause they got your attention either you know or don't you believe or you won't I'm chase God I don't wanna reap what I sow how deep could I go addicted to the words that he wrote I constantly grow I'm pray that you will follow him though not I I'm nothing but a passenger a messenger telling you that God is everlasting and his love will strengthen ya for real any day could be your last peep it darkness all around you but you can't see it its no secret the worlds leading did you decide to leave him because your own grievance did you try to reach em if you do believe em matter of fact did you even make up your own mind this evening wake up God is teaching plus you still breathing and you ain't even thankful for real you handful ain't no time to pretend dude if hating is what you into that's why I recommend you the Holy spirit I will send you follow God befriend the truth before they end you ain't nothing else real only God is essential your life could be ruined think hard what you doing forever pursuing I'ma praise God till I'm fluent understand whatever happens with faith I'ma go through it.

They controlling you

Lord forgive me for my sins I repent once again this word is as much for me as it is as much for them and I want them to know in there mind spirit and soul that you are real and in control I'm just a servant playing my role we have to repent constantly and speak honestly passionately wait on the lord so we could see what he's got for our tree move with God make sure to tell em Jesus Christ is the gate they need to believe and have faith because God's the only way.

How many people died was it real was it fake was it planned was it plane do you believe what you saw or what they say is that the same people is it staged how did he pass away why is everybody leaving what's special about today why you gotta agree without checking for your self why they telling you what's inside without opening the shelf why they all saying this is bad but I see something worst why can't God show us life why is man such a curse how you figure that's what happened that's not what I saw but since everybody said the same story I guess I lost maybe your right maybe I should do what they say maybe I'm wrong yeah I kind of see it your way maybe I'm strong enough to make up my own mind today maybe the more you lie the more I see only God's is the way maybe 2 or 3 won't be fooled by what 30 people say even if you dealing from the bottom of the deck they'll still play the deaf dumb and blind the walking dead forever 1 million followers Jumping off the Brooklyn Bridge together it's cold put on this sweater in 90 degree weather go shopping it's the end the world my fella don't tell him just buy some purses there on sale and it's worth it don't pay your phone you need Jordan's go stand online it will perfect with the new jeans that surfaced why is everybody cursing are all cops racist if your fat or you worthless they ugly she's hot don't get married stay single why being Christian is hard and why being bad is simple its mind control the world following the devils lies in the making same reason God asked you who told you was naked ain't no time for faking choose God not satan God saves plus he's calling you wake up they controlling you.

CHAPTER 6

Where your faith at

Lord forgive me for my sins I repent once again this word is as much for me as it is as much for them and I want them to know in there mind spirit and soul that you are real and in control I'm just a servant playing my role we have to repent constantly and speak honestly passionately wait on the lord so we could see what he's got for our tree move with God make sure to tell em Jesus Christ is the gate they need to believe and have faith because God's the only way.

I see them crying inside dying because of bad choices bad men bad people with no love but God's the surgeon no faith so they chose to stay with a bunch of curses he said that he'll change she thought he was worth it who picked em God or you calm down don't get nervous I'm talking trying to do some soul searching cause none of us or perfect but through God I'm learning these things are concerning I don't wanna see you burning you being what you wanna be running manually running solo no it all syndrome a catastrophe you don't need instructions to see but you on a balance beam who gave you your eyes and ears to hear do it gradually ask for he who you need G.o.d. let him lead so you won't be running around aimlessly still arguing fighting protesting and debating crying over Hillary upset trump made it marching to the white house trying to make a statement but if you had faith in God you would honor his arrangements only God does the changing maintaining and creating but since you don't know him you still just hating glory to God put your faith in him not on no other things cause people could play with people but not with the true king believe I really hope this is getting through if God made you doesn't he know what best you listen God's greater the undertaker don't know when your day is up now or later he's the alpha and omega the true savior he knows the beginning and the end so get your faith up woe to the faithless stand up Christ will come back if you really believe in God show me where your faith at.

Such a waste

Lord forgive me for my sins I repent once again this word is as much for me as it is as much for them and I want them to know in there mind spirit and soul that you are real and in control I'm just a servant playing my role we have to repent constantly and speak honestly passionately wait on the lord so we could see what he's got for our tree move with God make sure to tell em Jesus Christ is the gate they need to believe and have faith because God's the only way.

Let God be your supplier you running around disrespecting the messiah smoking drinking partying to the lake of fire everything you doing programmed to live foolish you just wasting your life and your time until your ruined towards the end you'll see you was destined for more but didn't surrender your God's invention live through him covered by the blood and his protection but you just follow the wicked world and you don't pay attention chasing everything else when Christ is the resurrection nothing goes with you back to dust you return your spirit goes to God and if your rejected your soul will burn when will you learn not to drink from the devils nectar not never the taste is great but filled with poison the soul collector going extra to try to get ya inhale this lecture yes sir only Christ will protect ya why live for this world when God was your investor such a crime committed against the kingdom that was out of line let me refresh your mind the sacrifice of Christ is why you shine living on borrowed time but you turn your face on a dime then use it to clean your dirty laundry but only God can clean your mind why struggle for the wrong reasons to lose all at the end how you fight for the wrong things plus your a follower of men a trillion dollars a standing ovation a thousand praises and no salvation and no right answers when you face em you came into this world naked please tell me what did you do with the time you was given preach to others help your brothers speak of God or just selfishly living live for God or loose your place he's the one you gonna face don't believe the devil lies without God this world is such a waste.

I'm not going with you

Lord forgive me for my sins I repent once again this word is as much for me as it is as much for them and I want them to know in there mind spirit and soul that you are real and in control I'm just a servant playing my role we have to repent constantly and speak honestly passionately wait on the lord so we could see what he's got for our tree move with God make sure to tell em Jesus Christ is the gate they need to believe and have faith because God's the only way.

I'm blessed glory to God by grace I'm still here real talk I don't deserve it by his blood I was purchased God loves me even though I'm a filthy rag working and I'm hurting I love you and Jesus is worth it but your blinded by the world's lies living without Christ the devils taking you down let God be your guide I pray for you everyday I pray that you would find his way please listen I'm really grieving for you today for real I wanna give you what I know what I feel what I've learned I'm praying for your salvation I'm concerned I hope that you understand I hope that you repent my man I hope she gets this clear I'm hoping your lizard ears hear I know that life is hard I know it's hard to believe I know you caught up but I'm hoping that you receive I care I feel for you I love you and tear for you but I can't force anything so let me be clear to you not my kids not my brother or my sisters or my mother is gonna keep me from God or the Comforter the blood covers the saints suffer ain't no other but Jesus Christ the savior above all so I'ma stand tall and God is who I'ma call I'm growing it's official I love you and I miss you and I'll do my best to help you but I ain't going with you.

God is all you need

Lord forgive me for my sins I repent once again this word is as much for me as it is as much for them and I want them to know in there mind spirit and soul that you are real and in control I'm just a servant playing my role we have to repent constantly and speak honestly passionately wait on the lord so we could see what he's got for our tree move with God make sure to tell em Jesus Christ is the gate they need to believe and have faith because God's the only way.

Keep letting the devil play with you the world Got a trade for you got you believing there's a better plan a better way for you I'm staying lose or draw pain or fame Christ the name whatever tribulation through sunshine and rain I'm in the field and you need to know only God is real the devil a liar trying to offer you a fake deal but God is the supplier trying to get your spirits higher he the one to admire but when its time for church you tired busy money chasing wired just trying to get flyer you and all that gold could melt in the lake of fire believe God is it don't sell God for nothing you bugging the word is clear but people be fronting steady Jumping for whatever crazy deal the beast give em they losing straight blinded check the mirror you ruined look around stop think what are you doing don't even love your kids you put em in the same situation you in let God light the way before you pass away such a shame to gain the world but to end up in flames not the way running from your pops but then you want change all the way trying to run your life like you in charge but here comes the pain listen if God don't break you prepare you then remake you on the front line for the devil to come take you your wasting your time with no time for God who made you and I did it before for a long time so I could relate true now I got my focus on Christ that's our lord forgot the world I know who to die for go hard try God your loss if you choose to stay lost as for me to continue best decision made by far God's who I cry for open up your eyeballs you sleep and your worth more then a couple dollars bruh it's not a game you need God to succeed let God take the lead because God is all you need.

God over feelings

Lord forgive me for my sins I repent once again this word is as much for me as it is as much for them and I want them to know

in there mind spirit and soul that you are real and in control I'm just a servant playing my role we have to repent constantly and speak honestly passionately wait on the lord so we could see what he's got for our tree move with God make sure to tell em Jesus Christ is the gate they need to believe and have faith because God's the only way.

You mad but won't submit you going against the ship the ark because your heart and the lies the devil talk going against your own cause you having a tough time and you been around God but refuse to pay em any mind and as others co sign your crime God will shine you fighting against the lord cause you don't believe and that's fine but soon you will hear it and soon you will fear it and you can't fight God or stop the Holy Spirit so when you get touched you gonna be in trouble dude but the lords plans are not to harm you but to prosper you and I hear you all men are bad cause God didn't choose them you did the devil confused you now it's hate men I'm getting a chick you two steps shy or you are already kissing her lips blasphemy the devil won't everything backwards kid you will see hopefully if it's not to late to agree with the truth and that's Christ are you feeling me and every other day the devil trying to get rid of you and me and you will be losing without G.o.d keep following the world you'll see what disaster really means same ol serpent with poison stay hurting and stay lurking trying to bring back Sodom and Gomorrah but God's always working It's easy to blame everyone but not look in the mirror it's easy to play the victim but God's words are clearer I hear ya should I chase you as you walk away this time you left me but I'm the one to blame everyday cause my past is up to date but God tossed my pass away so I could follow him today it's cool I'll continue to pray we wasn't brought up in the word so the world lead us astray if

ANGELO MELENDEZ

God didn't change me I would of been partying all day Yahweh Glory to God I'ma go hard and there ain't no Santa so read this Jesus card stop lying and stop faking ya love God from a distance won't follow the word and live it but you say you a Christian with no forgiveness and glorifying what you done in existence but done nothing for kingdom in which book ya name gonna be written I forgive you stop tripping open your ears and listen I'ma follow Christ he's life and it's God over feelings.

CHAPTER 7

who you dying for

Lord forgive me for my sins I repent once again this word is as much for me as it is as much for them and I want them to know in there mind spirit and soul that you are real and in control I'm just a servant playing my role we have to repent constantly and speak honestly passionately wait on the lord so we could see what he's got for our tree move with God make sure to tell em Jesus Christ is the gate they need to believe and have faith because God's the only way.

oh man blasphemy got you hyped all over again following demonic trends till you reach your end you can't live without your phone you can't live without spending you can't live without drugs the world is your God keeping you tempted I'm climbing for Lord my life is his forever you busy chasing money just so you could look better so called go getter but you not clever blinded by the darkness rejecting your own treasure without God in your center trying to get fresher following the world being mislead by whatever let me tell ya you really lost my fella it's time repent it's time to surrender understand man dang man you dictated by fame and I'm praising his holy name and he's the one in command fam he's constantly saving you but you and him are strangers you trying you stay lit I'm on fire the holy spirit changes and no matter how much you hate I'm still gonna love my neighbors and no one can get over on God the creator Glory to God listen God is life praise him never stop he the bread of life is Christ without em you in danger catch me hugging the bible while you hug the block pushing rock for me water flows out I'm drinking you understand me not and I love ya I pray daily this what Christ got me use to but ya say I'm scared I'm the sucker but the devil talk through you weak without em you need God just like I do you just don't know no better homie you was lied too you living for money ring jewels rims and things I'm trying to sing for him cause I live through him I'm trying to ride for him we alive cause him I'm signed to him ya dying for the wrong reasons like the color of skin he's coming again you'll see what kind of trouble you in keep partying sin leads to hell thinking you gonna win I'm living my life for Christ for sure he's pure but you living for the world take a look who you dying for.

Happy New Year!!!

God knows best

Lord forgive me for my sins I repent once again this word is as much for me as it is as much for them and I want them to know in there mind spirit and soul that you are real and in control I'm just a servant playing my role we have to repent constantly and speak honestly passionately wait on the lord so we could see what he's got for our tree move with God make sure to tell em Jesus Christ is the gate they need to believe and have faith because God's the only way.

I promise this is love and I'm truly concerned a hater will stay quiet and just let you burn this my chance to speak the truth to your heart I got a flashlight bright why would I leave you in the dark I thought I was done lost in the streets playing for keeps chasing money with greed a drug dealer asleep a drug addict full of deceit I was the worst I could be a destroyer a thief surrounded by darkness so incomplete praise the Lord that's in me I'm gonna continue to pray cause being gay the new wave they be proud to say I have a evil spirit in me they get applause and celebrate receive awards and praise huh devils lies today such a beautiful waste a true liar but I'm fishing please don't listen when he was casted out of heaven he took angels with him we have been separate forever we need to come together we only think that we can't but God knows better some don't make it to next year hope your here I pray I'm trying to leave with God but ya'll trying to stay I will leave it in God's hands he'll carry me all the way hands up scream loud hallelujah all day cast out what I can't defeat keep me away from the enemy changed my life my views now I pray and I preach I had to go through all of it so I know how to speak so Jesus loves you now put that on repeat you remind me of me not listening to anything wake up change for your son's daughters nephews or niece please understand the cross we don't deserve to breathe we are weak he took our place for all sins indeed mercy and grace repent to him constantly we owe a debt we can't pay no words you could say just live your life for Christ have faith fast and praise there's nothing you control dirt just blows away especially if you not firm with God Nowadays power plays are set to try to turn my face never try again I won't lose my faith I ain't blaming nothing I change nothing prayers are sent to lord he'll rearrange the fronting switch who's stunting knock you off your horse you bluffing change your mind like Paul God's the ruler you bugging understand this he's the beginning and the end you link repent follow God he'll change the way that you think new year new ears hope you listen to this you need an encounter with the lord he's the doctor you're sick only Christ got the answers to light up your eclipse hypocrites reverse the curses from your wicked lips you missed the blood and armor all on my chest I'm nothing without Jesus Christ and God knows best.

its Possible love

Lord forgive me for my sins I repent once again this word is as much for me as it is as much for them and I want them to know in there mind spirit and soul that you are real and in control I'm just a servant playing my role we have to repent constantly and speak honestly passionately wait on the lord so we could see what he's got for our tree move with God make sure to tell em Jesus Christ is the gate they need to believe and have faith because God's the only way.

My brother down that dark road alone God's showing the true path you blinded by everything you don't really understand bad your lips are wicked but money got feeling exquisite you only see destruction surrounded by demolitions you need reconstruction the devil took your vision and even though you're dying you still refuse to listen What God sees isn't what you see if he chose me your broken mirror you need to fix it look closely be careful with who you dancing what you worry about could be answered that the lord will cut out that cancer where your faith at when it happens one Rock Goliath stay back killing hate facts pain retracts you can't believe the truth till he play it back my beautiful women I believe the king sent them but the world got your mind clouded and you won't represent him Jesus loves you wants to prosper you with love and happiness but the devils craftiness got you walking around sad and sick you choose the bad over good your partner killing you lost in room full of fake love and doom they say love is blind I say your out your mind shouldn't Jesus the messiah now what's best for you to find true love something precious when nurtured and treated right will blossom to a beautiful woman do you believe in his light I believe under all the pain and hurt that you've gone through there's a breakthrough there's a light to help you to take you to new heights with new life repent be born through Christ we need that love because God is love all the time right so feel his touch and this spiritual hug I promise God is all and all is possible love.

Gracious time

Lord forgive me for my sins I repent once again this word is as much for me as it is as much for them and I want them to know in there mind spirit and soul that you are real and in control I'm just a servant playing my role we have to repent constantly and speak honestly passionately wait on the lord so we could see what he's got for our tree move with God make sure to tell em Jesus Christ is the gate they need to believe and have faith because God's the only way.

Thank you lord for giving us one of the Greatest costly Gifts that we didn't deserve your love has me convinced thank you lord for giving us time through the blood of Christ you gave us time to redesign time to fall in line time to break the vicious generational curse of pain and hurt time so that we can wake up and change the whole earth time knowing that you are the truth the way and the life time to change our ways time to repent and do it right time to start again time to avoid hell time so that we can live the life you gave us for you and not for ourselves time to get close to you like we supposed to time so that we can pray for others to know you time I was lost and you took out time to find me time to find her or him choose wisely time to believe in you with all our hearts time for you to step into the light and leave the dark time so now we can raise a new generation of Christians that follow and preach your word everyday and listen lord thank you lord you are the one I'ma mention so merciful to us way beyond comprehension and I just want to give you all the Glory Forever thanks for the time I won't let go of you never but time is running out soon please Christians stay on your grind once again I thank you God for all your Gracious time.

I know he's with me

Lord forgive me for my sins I repent once again this word is as much for me as it is as much for them and I want them to know in there mind spirit and soul that you are real and in control I'm just a servant playing my role we have to repent constantly and speak honestly passionately wait on the lord so we could see what he's got for our tree move with God make sure to tell em Jesus Christ is the gate they need to believe and have faith because God's the only way.

Actually when I didn't follow him he protected me while I disrespected him he still was helping me through everything I went through he was there my pain was a lesson to learn so I can share my corrupted mind was an experience that led to my deliverance was confused without God no love and no significance I couldn't hold me chased everything the streets told me was defeated slowly by the enemy but God still chose me what mercy smiling while dying if you would've looked closely not knowing Hells creeping thought money was my trophy I never cared to know him but he's the one that knows me and trust me he knows you too and soon he will show you you'll see might not be now might not be later I just hope for your sake you don't miss that call from your creator because his loves greater then all paper yup I'm talking brown paper bags with green paper and roll paper the one to change haters from dark Vader to loving thy neighbors the world destroying many and God's the real educator so I'ma continue to pray and keep my vision on the lord I suggest you do the same only Christ is the cure for your sickness most being led to destruction even Christians vanity is there witness the devils a lying technician a decision has to be made by you and God will represent you but you disrespect God daily destroying your own temple type a stuff that you into I'm not trying to offend you I've been there for years a slave to my own corrupted mentals please I do know the world's dreams are a disease got you chasing all your wants but God will give you what you need but let me let ya know this real love though one day you'll see the light I just hope you don't let it go trust that I got your best interests a messenger doing God's Business but he's the one you need to make it through please listen look at everything you do understand God's the truth realize your whole life darkness been telling what to do I've changed glory to God to father and his son plus the holy spirit without them I would've been done won't forget where he saved me from I'll never forget that he hung and the blood he shed for us all now this is outcome me telling you to wake up and believe you disobedient and he's still loves you but I know he's with me.

CHAPTER 8

it's tough believe

Lord forgive me for my sins I repent once again this word is as much for me as it is as much for them and I want them to know in there mind spirit and soul that you are real and in control I'm just a servant playing my role we have to repent constantly and speak honestly passionately wait on the lord so we could see what he's got for our tree move with God make sure to tell em Jesus Christ is the gate they need to believe and have faith because God's the only way.

I thank you lord for picking me up when I fall from victory we need you I'm so sick of me diligently relying that your grace sufficiently keeps lifting me the trinity is everything we need some are from your presence got me sad on my knees I pray for forgiveness sorry I disobey your lead nobody is good only God please Believe I'm walking God's official indeed I'm still surrounded by the darkness and the heartless cause the world don't change the holy spirit just converts kid and protects you from the serpent and the evil from that person fighting your flesh worsens situations keep birthing fighting demons in the surface this walk is hard but worth it to worship the one true God that's perfect our life was purchased by Christ on the cross why you nervous your disobedience got me nauseous of course there's no going back for me he proved my purpose I'm his servant while you blind to fact dodging churches and I ain't got no time for games you deserve this I pray for your encounter surrender to G.o.d I'm strong sometimes but love matters get me weak so also pray for me I don't want to see defeat I'm fighting can't you see this walk is tough believe.

What's it for

Lord forgive me for my sins I repent once again this word is as much for me as it is as much for them and I want them to know in there mind spirit and soul that you are real and in control I'm just a servant playing my role we have to repent constantly and speak honestly passionately wait on the lord so we could see what he's got for our tree move with God make sure to tell em Jesus Christ is the gate they need to believe and have faith because God's the only way.

All the decisions that you make aren't for God who was it for living selfish without God tell me what's it for are you bringing glory to God tell me what's it for do your moves honor God tell me what's it for wrong door wrong path bad decision with a laugh evil divides so you don't grow this ain't a typo you a psycho you think you on point in a vicious cycle so I write you telling you the devils lies you gotta fight through but you deaf dumb you no rest guided by the world and flesh following behind other men darkness moves you every step plus you think that your correct saying oh I believe in God such disrespect you aint following his laws yall do the opposite think ya gonna win everything is money lit the night life the party click ya never stop destroying temple ya looking really sick real change comes from God hope you really getting me you ain't changed you still trapped inside of party city mentally go ahead threaten me the truth hurts your integrity I'm sorry but I love you and you need help desperately God the only way hands up get on your knees today word up time to surrender man up to the lord homie that's what's up look back where you at think back but relax your whole life you've been trash without Christ with no map no light no truth just devil hyping you dummy you followed the world that was directed by who satan yes I did it too wake up I'm talking dude I rebuke the devil and all his works trying to destroy all of you this ain't game man stop playing why you chose your own way and why you think getting money is changing why she like you for the doe you came with just saying why she think money is all why she lost help her bro step in protect her you be the real Adam you was supposed know step in reject the serpent follow Christ risen hope she broken too can't you see her life is crying though forgive me if I don't believe enough to put her on her feet bring her close to God so he can wipe away her vanity sorry ma but this the truth yup the devil got you too you sitting up there confused trying to be the man now you lose even worst spreading your legs just to be on top of men taking what can so then you can slander them once again the devils path is really lit leading you to Lake you feeling it not for you cause you said you believe in God in same breath hypocrite blinded by the darkness quit check out who you walking with Go live and see inside your self before you poison all of them only God can give you health only Christ can break the spell cause your sick you left him ya'll lost without him make the call chose for yourself now you fall stuck with the wrong dude for sure where he's leading you to planet lost but he a boss forget the cross you love him more then God of course keep making decisions for applause who you thought that you was I'm asking one question what's it for.

It's all our fault

Lord forgive me for my sins I repent once again this word is as much for me as it is as much for them and I want them to know in there mind spirit and soul that you are real and in control I'm just a servant playing my role we have to repent constantly and speak honestly passionately wait on the lord so we could see what he's got for our tree move with God make sure to tell em Jesus Christ is the gate they need to believe and have faith because God's the only way.

We did it the constant fall of man started the madness now it's to late we destroyed our own race chasing money not faith destroyed our own kids lives with racism and lies another dead baby oh my another child cries we're blind to our own mirror bad decisions to pull the trigger and instead of turning to God we follow men open your ears up I pray ya'll sacrifice for what's wrong everyday and the blood Jesus spilled means nothing to most of ya'll today lack of knowledge got you in prison keep on following the wicked upset with your own struggle but you still refuse to listen we them haters we them crabs in barrel without God we ugly most of us unjust and quickly sellout for money the root of all make you lose it all but Jesus is who I'ma call before or after I fall I'ma worship God for sure he's pure the doctrine never change is us acting insane we believe the devils lies then everybody else's the blame we're lost we're in trouble now she wears the pants trying to hustle and straight girls still waiting for a tall, faithful ,rich man with muscles I'ma make ya'll say uncle nah I'ma make ya'll say Jesus because your life has been a lie without him you in pieces let God choose for you let God's moves control you instead of making lustful decisions that are all bad for you are you good got money a house and car how lovely your comfortable in a cell full of sins headed to hell what a trap oh well you never cared for the creator go ahead live it up don't forget to thank the devil later God's greater believe he's still waiting for you player he'll receive you just repent on your knees wholeheartedly and believe God will raise your spirits accordingly to his will and your needs and your life will start to make sense spiritually so please surrender to God go ahead step forth change your thoughts put God first of course and no matter what happens remember it's all our fault.

Narrow is the gate to salvation

Lord forgive me for my sins I repent once again this word is as much for me as it is as much for them and I want them to know in there mind spirit and soul that you are real and in control I'm just a servant playing my role we have to repent constantly and speak honestly passionately wait on the lord so we could see what he's got for our tree move with God make sure to tell em Jesus Christ is the gate they need to believe and have faith because God's the only way.

They busy following people chasing fame and money they telling us do what you want got our kids sexually confused as they growing up guy or chick girl or slut taught to bust a nut and run steal and fight man or punk 4 against 1 getting jumped grab a gun kill or be killed slap her up disrespect your temple you disrespecting God that's not what's up Crips and bloods smoking trees taking E pills got you messing up chasing money got ya falling down ain't nobody looking up open your eyes evil is leading in everyway broad is the gate to temptation killing ya everyday another life to waste another brother passed away cause nobody taught em about the love of Christ today party all day lost without faith they full of hate no time for God no escape racism going both ways they telling you it's to late big bang theory now we apes another lie another fake what to do kneel and pray the word of God is the truth ok God's not for play prince of peace gave you life wake up and see his sacrifice fight what's wrong do what's right love God with all your might live for him the one to trust let his blood cover you up don't be fooled by what you see believe in God let him lead don't be like the world they got you following the enemy put down the Hennessy they trying to make you sin regularly stay in the word depart from sin or you'll never be heavenly unless you repent and change your whole pedigree start praising because the devil got most of ya'll hell-raising broad is the gate to destruction narrow is the gate to salvation.

There will be justice for us

Lord forgive me for my sins I repent once again this word is as much for me as it is as much for them and I want them to know in there mind spirit and soul that you are real and in control I'm just a servant playing my role we have to repent constantly and speak honestly passionately wait on the lord so we could see what he's got for our tree move with God make sure to tell em Jesus Christ is the gate they need to believe and have faith because God's the only way.

Keep thinking that you good keep thinking you ok following the world being misled all day keep saying you believe in God not following his rules you just living for yourself living a life for fools I can't applaud your dealings with evil that mislead you I don't wanna see lost forever if I could lead you to Christ forget your Peoples they be the ones to leave you after they hyped you to bang back everybody ran track your left stranded bleeding or locked up not knowing where your man's at I can't stand that but Jesus loves you understand that in advance jack everybody wants heaven without the discipline they don't live for God but they believe they getting in they rather believe the devils lies cause they can't be obedient cowards fake gangsters the real challenge is to live for him real men pray and worship real men stay in churches real man treat a girl perfect because they know her worth kid they marry a princess before they touch her on purpose they following God's laws they ain't following the serpent without Christ your life is just a lie look beyond the surface you following the world not the word go to service without his presence you absurd plus Jesus don't deserve this you utterly opposed to the real living wordless running around hating another lost person forgetting that you we're purchase you'll end up in hells furnace everything is an excuse to avoid the truth since your youth you've been lied to and the time the lord has given you ya'll just misuse it won't let him guide you thinking he not watching thinking you won't be touched thinking you could live how you want but there will be justice for us so give God everything you have cause there will be justice for us whether good or bad there will be justice for us.

POEMS AND STORIES

God's daughters

Lord forgive me for my sins I repent once again this word is as much for me as it is as much for them and I want them to know in there mind spirit and soul that you are real and in control I'm just a servant playing my role we have to repent constantly and speak honestly passionately wait on the lord so we could see what he's got for our tree move with God make sure to tell em Jesus Christ is the gate they need to believe and have faith because God's the only way.

Your God's daughter full of his spirit that's what I should see I believe in our God trust he loves you and me don't let nothing or no one change your mind or spirit stay right with the lord forever continue to live it if it doesn't Glorify God then it's gotta hit the road if it's not for God's glory then you gotta let it go remember if it's pulling away from the lord how will you grow there's a lot of God's work to do we gotta continue to flow your partner should speak life to you guided by the lord bring you closer God a love that will never divorce he should want to help you protect you and ya both pray for each other together for God's glory steady helping each other ya won't fade won't fold forget what they say God is in control evil will always try but God runs the show don't to listen to the world's craziness keep on learning keep growing uplifting and church preaching keeping the Holy Spirit burning his word and his gifts are what make you beautiful not make up jewels or clothes or the disobedient things that you do the Holy Spirits why ya should love each other choose each other and trust each other plus ya wont mess up on God the only one that can judge others ya should want nothing but the best for ya God's blessings never miss he'll always lead the way he got you this far if you are his never forget Jesus loves you and God is a God of order always remember who you are your one of God's daughters.

Steal, Kill, and Destroy

Lord forgive me for my sins I repent once again this word is as much for me as it is as much for them and I want them to know in there mind spirit and soul that you are real and in control I'm just a servant playing my role we have to repent constantly and speak honestly passionately wait on the lord so we could see what he's got for our tree move with God make sure to tell em Jesus Christ is the gate they need to believe and have faith because God's the only way.

Pick your poison since I'm chosen the devil haunts me and wants me got me choosing from either the bad or the ugly but with God I change the sentence and create a different question praying to lord puts me in a different section I see you dealing and stealing my blessings more threatening with weapons harassing me with your minions praying I start sinning thinking you Winning angry cause I'm still praising not changing hating creating corruption with every situation killing me softly going deep with the hateration throwing stones I'll build a wall you throwing them for me to fall more traps so I could fail more tricks to make me trip more passageways to hell homie you ain't slick oh well glory to God I will take it and smile you trying to kill my spirit even using my child a family member or a friend but I'm walking again no weapon formed against me shall prosper till the end I'ma worship Follow God cause he's perfect everything works for the best guaranteed it's all worth it fallen but not destroyed picked up when I'm annoyed uplifted by Christ you ain't stealing my joy oh boy I see you destroying others around me so I could suffer but the lord gives me strength to get through and his blood covers I love ya but I'm sorry you won't be taken me trying to put my faith to sleep with God I'm never weak trying to make me follow you breaking me hoping I fall apart aimlessly God's protecting me the lord has awaken me showed me your intentions daily now I could walk off patiently won't change my melody God still the remedy God still the energy and he's the centerpiece and the air I breath won't catch me hating faking or changing cause of the enemy playing games but with Christ I'm no toy the enemy only here to steal , kill and destroy.

Vision on God

Lord forgive me for my sins I repent once again this word is as much for me as it is as much for them and I want them to know in there mind spirit and soul that you are real and in control I'm just a servant playing my role we have to repent constantly and speak honestly passionately wait on the lord so we could see what he's got for our tree move with God make sure to tell em Jesus Christ is the gate they need to believe and have faith because God's the only way.

The devil got you making bad choices in the darkness without voices or scriptures none believers none listeners end up in the mix with the trickster the wrong way bad decisions on a mission walking with the wrong people put your trust in pure evil where is it gonna lead you in love not knowing true intentions or evil infections since you refuse to believe in God suffer the consequences there tremendous repent choose God he's the answer don't run keep your two eyes on lord no matter what's being done certain people some destroyers are spiritually killing for fun it's in there nature taught to be racist taught be hating taught to be selfishly living transformed to disrespect the scriptures that we're God given but you could be forgiven and God can Change your thinking please understand Jesus Christ is my religion you need a heart of flesh to break that stone that got you tripping let these words be the ignition there free no admission they got you hating forever gone growing up wrong daughters and sons nothing good comes out of a wicked Tung there spirit is done so tell me what's it gonna be victory or defeat if you don't plant the seed to your seed it will grow up a creep if you don't instruct it in the word the child will grow up to mislead cause once the world begin to teach they gonna be out your reach evil taught in the streets it's gonna be hard to compete let God lead from the start so they could know how to seek the lords presence every day so they could fight no retreat no surrender only to Christ hear the words that I speak with God they will be strong without God they'll be weak break the cycle make a change the devils playing for keeps you could catch me close to God battling on my knees look at what you see God's the one that we need stay focused go hard keep your vision on God.

What's yours

Lord forgive me for my sins I repent once again this word is as much for me as it is as much for them and I want them to know

in there mind spirit and soul that you are real and in control I'm just a servant playing my role we have to repent constantly and speak honestly passionately wait on the lord so we could see what he's got for our tree move with God make sure to tell em Jesus Christ is the gate they need to believe and have faith because God's the only way.

You have the right to worship Christ for life with all your might and no one nobody no demon no devil could dim your light our stop are take away your ability to serve the lord our lord the king of glory with God the devils lies bore me our merciful king praise him forever and ever full of joy full power to resist the devil whenever this world is mostly destroyed but I'm full of the holy spirit how you denied your lord and savior his blood and presence should be remembered and I aint talking Easter I ain't talking Christmas in December I'm mean daily worship to God the only one to mention the one and only on the throne he'll never leave you alone you refuse to follow God but want him to bring your spirit home where you at living wrong disrespecting God's steps in the dark searching for death without God his word you neglect the world is out of order but the lord keeps me correct while you reject his word you don't accept but he's the one that gave you breath the first Adam fell the second man was Christ defeated death and the devil with skin and bones paid a price a sacrifice for your life get up if God with you keep pushing don't let them get you father of lies stealing your joy trying to break you stand up resist evil hands high Jesus we need you it's time to keep fighting time to overcome the deceitful praise and all glory to our lord keep walking tall anointed by his presence worship God take back what's yours.

ANGELO MELENDEZ

Destroying Love

Lord forgive me for my sins I repent once again this word is as much for me as it is as much for them and I want them to know in there mind spirit and soul that you are real and in control I'm just a servant playing my role we have to repent constantly and speak honestly passionately wait on the lord so we could see what he's got for our tree move with God make sure to tell em Jesus Christ is the gate they need to believe and have faith because God's the only way.

Destroying love when you supposed to lead her not abuse her she getting sick and tired of your excuses you damaging love everyone loses the lord gave you a gift and you just misuse it leaving her unrecognizable everybody is like who's this nothing left but cuts and bruises what if it was your sis but then you sorry again and she forgive again sometimes it's drugs or that bottle that got you lifting your hands the devils lies got you loss ain't no need to pretend that's your partner not your personal punching bag my friend she was created to bring life and you ain't treating her right so was your mom's if they did that to her you've be tight she's beautiful in everyway and you dimming her light killing her right plus your daughter might pay the price what you thinking this is why we need the lords traditions to make you into the Adam that's leads with love and vision that puts his wife first after Christ bringing paradise he appreciates life she proud to be his only wife getting through with sacrifice he uplifting her day and night not beating her down destroying her spirit just killing her life and it's you that she's trusting that's part of the problem that's disgusting ladies choose God so he can lead you to your husband fellas let God show you how to be a man before judgment and maybe we'll make a change that go from zero to hundreds and maybe God is love will spread throughout the public and maybe just maybe then our kids will learn something instead of destroying love in front of them like nothing.

We're all killers

Not one is good no not one I don't care where you from we all need Jesus the air to our lungs we make decisions unaware of consequences we don't care we don't see our harm we step over people to get there how you figure haa if I sold you drugs I was a killer if I gave you liquor and you crashed and died I pulled the trigger if you didint die I'm still causing your death if I'm not guiding you to christ towards who em I guiding you then towards lucy you could smoke her or touch her body she's juicy he ain't coming with a pitchfork and horns excuse me I set the tone to your crisis when I told you pop off told you to hit it and quit it be strong not soft she too young hold on she looked around you was gone now that baby born in the dumpster you don't think you wrong the type of ignition that destroys intuition with repetition sins taught through communication but you blame it on the system you tripping in the streets and the world call it living chasing money power and sex and then your son end up in prison or dead but who he following your pride you need too be swallowing if you ain't bringing people to christ you sacrificing them passing sinful mind diseases everytime you hyping em sound like a killer to me you told them they don't belong the way you treated them in church showed no love what's going on you killed them spiritually so they left the church torn right into the devil's grasp there death is your lost we supposed to aspire and take everybody higher the only party that's gonna be lit is the one in the lake of fire check your steps before you take em watch your mouth or you'll forsake em give your life to christ so lifes decision he'll help you make em Jesus Christ is the light get him and dont let it Flicker be careful who you kill right now we're all killers.

Don't let the devil/world scare you

Such lies and waste of time to dim your shine you could lose the whole world today but keep christ inside they gonna tell you what to fight for so could ignore the God's laws don't let the devil tell you your life is more important then the lord like you can't loose her or you can't loose him the pastor gotta preach whether you leave the church or decide to stay in Sing and just cause a man or woman did you dirty I know that's sad the devil used the fear of getting hurt again now you mad but that dont mean everyone's bad and you gotta turn drag or be lesbian which is an abomination to our dad our heavenly Father ya letting the devil take ya down that path and left alone in the darkness and devil gonna laugh once again if you ain't following I gotta keep moving I believe God even if my kids don't believe what I'm doing but the devils lies come through just bringing confusion drugs make everything better sex calmness and music what your pursuing popularity is an addiction the devil got you cruising promoting foolishness look at me I'm gangsta tell me what or you proving or promoting your beauty and body the attentions amusing you forgot about the word of God and got a million excuses but who you bruising yourself and God's watching your movement and the devil got you scared so you continue to ruin putting things over God so who's really loosing won't be me I'ma stand with christ I can't do it take the world with everything in it for me God I'm choosing listen close stand firm with God whatever you do stay connected don't let the devil/ world scare you. Amen!

Now I know better

Lord forgive me for my sins I repent once again this word is as much for me as it is as much for them and I want them to know in there mind spirit and soul that you are real and in control I'm just a servant playing my role we have to repent constantly and speak honestly passionately wait on the lord so we could see what he's got for our tree move with God make sure to tell em Jesus christ is the gate they need to believe and have faith because God's the only way.

I know what you need I know how to be it's clearer now right or wrong makes so much sense to me I'm driven by God's work he's my life my inspiration the one true God of innovation I pray you are on good terms when you face him we will never come close that's no exaggeration so I'ma Glorify his life contributions to all nations I'm trying to help you through we are such a loss generation rasicm got you running around hating if my actions through life some how reach your brain dude and opens up your mind and begins to change you Glory to God if he renames you its more important than fame you know it is true so you could praise his name too and finally understand why you came too if me telling you Jesus loves you could frame you and rearrange you so you realize and repent change your world follow him understand that the devil got the world sick with lies and tricks trust me I was in frontline and I aint proud of it had me buggin out while Jesus was steady calling me I doubted him but now God's my rock the one to treasure I'ma Glorify his name forever there's no one better once he open up my heart and mind I could face whatever but now I know better wisdom makes you clever he's the one that will protect ya I thought I needed to party I thought I needed to drink I thought I needed to smoke I thought money was everything I thought I needed a bunch of women and expensive things but all we need is God the ruler of all things the problem is that God knows what we need man and the problem is that we never could see it and the problem is I'm telling you that you need him fam but the problem is will you really believe me to my sisters and my brothers what else can I tell ya don't be tricked like I was cause now I know better.

A Precious Jewel

Lord forgive me for my sins I repent once again this word is as much for me as it is as much for them and I want them to know in there mind spirit and soul that you are real and in control I'm just a servant playing my role we have to repent constantly and speak honestly passionately wait on the lord so we could see what he's got for our tree move with God make sure to tell em Jesus christ is the gate they need to believe and have faith because God's the only way.

How bad has it been how ugly they got you miserable it's critical and the devil takes advantage killing everything that's biblical probably ran to those with wrong answers spreading cancer more pain you see no way out from this disaster they keep you dirty filthy mistreated you for years plenty times they dropped you and left you you barely see clear they scrapped you they hit you they burned you they chipped you they cut you they pimped you they sold you they diss you they disrespected you they care nothing about you they gone now oh wow in your own tears you drown cause they cant be found they left you for brand new one that just came into to town they abused you but it happens so much that some get used to everything they going through like now it's the usual excuse you but I feel your pain and there's a

God you should've spoke to cause he brings change out with the bad in with the good the holy spirit only God can lead you to the right one no gimmicks cause God has no limits and before I finish I want you to listen your shine is infinite God said your a gift don't get it twisted get uplifted shifted so you won't be a victim that's all you missing look up through God's vision after all the damage after all the scars your still a star when treated right bright as ever thats what you are after all the wrong after everything they do with God you won't lose your still a precious Jewel.

Dishonor

Lord forgive me for my sins I repent once again this word is as much for me as it is as much for them and I want them to know in there mind spirit and soul that you are real and in control I'm just a servant playing my role we have to repent constantly and speak honestly passionately wait on the lord so we could see what he's got for our tree move with God make sure to tell em Jesus christ is the gate they need to believe and have faith because God's the only way.

Do you know what you doing do you really understand they got you disrespecting forcing God's hand bad man you pushing evil agendas that doe got your attention chasing money offenders knowing God is greater hater putting everything before the one that made ya disobedient to the creator these words are a sharp razor don't even want to try following every lie on the roof believing the devil telling you you could fly you twisted with nonsense I'm saying God got this you full of fibbs what God gives can't be bought Christ lives money ain't courage money ain't faith ain't life or salvation you ain't right following the hype epic fail all the way down to detail what you gonna do be buried in a gold casket then burn in hell I promise God is eternal the one you need to turn too whether I make it or don't put these words in your journal praise God the one that did what no one could so shout hallelujah plus a spiritual crushing we know nothing about hallelujah hurry up and put him in your house now hallelujah without the Comforter you on your way out hallelujah so get up on your knees praise the one true God get off that highway to hell is sabotage you living the wrong way you and your entourage forget a mask your whole life been camouflage thinking that you large thinking your a boss disrespecting the cross homie you really loss you in the dark with bad karma no armor get smarter the devil got you lost with all that Dishonor.

Quotes by Angelo Melendez A.K.A Veelito

Why is it easy to be bad hard to be good

Lord forgive me for my sins I repent once again this word is as much for me as it is as much for them and I want them to know in there mind spirit and soul that you are real and in control I'm just a servant playing my role we have to repent constantly and speak honestly passionately wait on the lord so we could see what he's got for our tree move with God make sure to tell em Jesus christ is the gate they need to believe and have faith because God's the only way.

Surrounded by temptation getting pulled in hyped up nonstop bad is bieng promoted and you follow like why not everybody got problems everyone is crazy everybody tough everything is shady are you acting following or depressed or a product of your inviorment I'm just inquiring the trick is that they lying man the problem is you buying it if not you trying it they painted a pic to choke you and your admiring it think about what they said you would go through now your rebellious cause what they told you plus since you don't believe who's gonna show you go chase everything in this world except God yeah we own you we got you either way you gonna condone whatever your prone too yes correct mind control and distractions false disasters you accept you still in the projects chasing money or chasing checks selfish last thing that they want is us put together so keep us apart through division there so clever nowadays you have to behave a certain way because of where you from or where you at and how you was raised they still pulling your strings such evil from within yes everybody sins but there's true Christians getting wins battling against there flesh and skin plus God's always amazing again miracles are done daily but he don't get spins only a few promoting him I hope your righteous when he get tight and shutdown the broadcast my friend when the dark comes light when judgement begins man up from disbelief follow God let him teach stop listening and following and be who God want you to be trying to conquer the world but at the end get tormented in defeat those that are cursed for generations and you following there lead wake up brother peep wake up you still sleep it's so easy to bad but to be good you gotta be unique everybody is a boss everybody wanna speak why can't we all be servents to God follow his word and read stand firm never leave live for him faithfully but everyone's for themselves just following deceit only if we could chase God like we chase money understood why is it easy to be bad but hard to be good.

Put him high

Lord forgive me for my sins I repent once again this word is as much for me as it is as much for them and I want them to know

in there mind spirit and soul that you are real and in control I'm just a servant playing my role we have to repent constantly and speak honestly passionately wait on the lord so we could see what he's got for our tree move with God make sure to tell em Jesus christ is the gate they need to believe and have faith because God's the only way.

His light shine bright his steps are all right I'm not worthy to breath his air I'm just happy to be here I pray that I could manage whatever he gives me to handle and none of us worthy enough to unlach his sandals I'm nothing without you lost in the world I've been there you gave me life and taught me right I'm surprised to be here forgive me for what I've done forgive me for living wrong your grace and mercy is above all your the reason I'm strong I'ma walk how I'm supposed to talk how I'm supposed to whether I reach heaven or not I'm forever praising through my vocals ain't nobody chose you you love us and most don't know you Jesus Christ is life the one you gotta get close to I pray that I could keep up with everything you teach us keep my vision on you and let nothing come between us thank you I'm breathing thank you I'm reading thank you because some that I know are now believing you lord you do it all everyday I need you more and even when I slip you pick me up after I fall now I'm humble and understand I never really had a plan until you opened up my eyes that's when my life began its all Christ none before he forever this my story he's the reason I'm never lonely to God be the glory I pray that you will rise and let God be your guide I don't know about you but I'ma put him high.

It's so Sad

Lord forgive me for my sins I repent once again this word is as much for me as it is as much for them and I want them to know in there mind spirit and soul that you are real and in control I'm just a servant playing my role we have to repent constantly and speak honestly passionately wait on the lord so we could see what he's got for our tree move with God make sure to tell em Jesus christ is the gate they need to believe and have faith because God's the only way.

I'm sorry that you don't know I feel bad everyday I hope and pray consistently that you will find your way he's waiting but you doubting they hating and you allowed it believing a hundred lies a day got your whole mind clouded instead of reaching yourself searching for self asking for some help you struggling ain't hard to tell your probably a prayer away but you give up constantly you follow your flesh your friends the world cool is the way you suffer but won't change your blind and far away from God. bless his holy name for sure I know he's real when the holy spirit penetrates certain ones get the shakes I just cry in everyway tears fall my heart breaks my soul burns hard to explain this feeling won't go away you can't get it nowhere it's such a shame a crime and you just need to experience it one time and you hooked God's real you shook up what's the deal you can't go back now he's watching yup time for you to heal the Lord is your redeemer your savior the creator and one thing that you think alot about is how to save your neighbor they need this God is amazing he's the one I'm chasing be true to God with obedience while plenty out there hating a lot are faking some debating a lot are praising alot are changing you missing blessings daily lost in the dark fading I can't go back Lord Jesus

Christ you need that I promise you he's real but you dont wanna believe that but these facts I went from ugly to worst to bad now following my dad nobody's good but I'ma Christian and a happy servant not to brag but all glory to God I'm relaxed on track I'm greatful for that cant be mad if God's all I have then I have all I'm glad but I worry for others on the wrong path I find it so sad.

Be careful with what you receive

Lord forgive me for my sins I repent once again this word is as much for me as it is as much for them and I want them to know in there mind spirit and soul that you are real and in control I'm just a servant playing my role we have to repent constantly and speak honestly passionately wait on the lord so we could see what he's got for our tree move with God make sure to tell em Jesus christ is the gate they need to believe and have faith because God's the only way.

The devil works with our desires with lies straight from a liar pushing you to the fire better reconnect your wire I hope your Wi-Fi connection to God don't expire mess around without prayer get caught in a crossfire that gift was a trap to distract and bring you back in fact it worked so well now your stuck and can't react got hyped cause of a check a house a car a pet anything so you could forget and begin to disrespect you can't even retrace your steps got you gassed today you don't even hardly pray plus you miles away it's a difference between being pulled towards God day and night and bieng misled taking away further from Christ how blind is love really I know it's tricky I won't be that silly no matter how pretty if she can't glorify God she can't ride with me I'm walking off casually she just don't fit me looking like J lo ,Bayonce or kim Kardashian it really don't matter nobody panicking God still with me and my armor still solid fam do what you want I'ma pray that you understand every snake ain't in the woods every lift ain't to the hood every gift aint good tell me you understood I'm stay on my knees praying God please open them up so they believe and be careful with what you receive.

So Peaceful

Lord forgive me for my sins I repent once again this word is as much for me as it is as much for them and I want them to know in there mind spirit and soul that you are real and in control I'm just a servant playing my role we have to repent constantly and speak honestly passionately wait on the lord so we could see what he's got for our tree move with God make sure to tell em Jesus christ is the gate they need to believe and have faith because God's the only way.

Through all the drama going on through all the pain I'm still in my lane through all the hate through all mistakes I'm smiling inside God is great even when I get upset it don't last it can't you bring me right back and tell me start again no statue no person no place or thing nothing from this world could bring peace only Jesus Christ is king a spiritual gift like this can't be bought with money I'm so peaceful most of the time I find stuff funny I'm so grateful because I believe in the God that's in me the one I pray you receive the bible is the key whether you cry or you bleed whether I stay or I leave I pray the lord intercedes in your life let him lead as for me I'ma reach I'ma praise I'ma speak God forever my life is in his hands can't you see let him reach you teach you without the Lord equals evil it's leathel we need him everyday be needful fearful we need to live for God not people at the end of the day I'm still joyful I'm covered so peaceful.

Joyful tears

Lord forgive me for my sins I repent once again this word is as much for me as it is as much for them and I want them to know in there mind spirit and soul that you are real and in control I'm just a servant playing my role we have to repent constantly and speak honestly passionately wait on the lord so we could see what he's got for our tree move with God make sure to tell em Jesus christ is the gate they need to believe and have faith because God's the only way.

Things just keep getting brighter our love gets tighter since I stepped out of the darkness been proving that I'm a fighter I pray to be an example not leading no one a stray I'm lit night and day Holy Spirit inside of me lord

I love you forever I really cant believe how generous you've been to me and I mean in everything I'm already in debt for life and your fulfilling my wants and needs and if I fall you give the strength to proceed only you know me only you know us in the lord I'ma trust till I go back to dust its must we going to praise you I love you and I'm Grateful Only God can change you dont wait till its to late true his love is faithful his grace awaits you in his arms he'll take you surrounded by his Angels he'll keep you stable and I will never stop forever and a day I want everything around me to praise your holy name blessed with no fear its raining blessings over here the word of God in my ears our God continues to draw near plus my Princess will soon appear hallelujah oh yea I cant ask for more I cry joyful tears.

The Bad one's

Lord forgive me for my sins I repent once again this word is as much for me as it is as much for them and I want them to know in there mind spirit and soul that you are real and in control I'm just a servant playing my role we have to repent constantly and speak honestly passionately wait on the lord so we could see what he's got for our tree move with God make sure to tell em Jesus christ is the gate they need to believe and have faith because God's the only way.

The word says that Gods the light of the world without him we're in darkness you aint gotta look to hard to see the heartless its us bieng swayed following the worlds ways selfish acts everyday they pull our strings and we play we all fall short of glory we're all usually naughty some Christians will ignore me lost in there own story we think we living proper we think we follow the father untill shorty holla or you fall to a dollar or whatever your trouble area is jealous envy anger hate or thee occasional fibb maybe you racist you was taught as kid same demon passed down from generation to generation you sick only Christ got the remedy he moving my man we listen to evil way more then we listen to him and she aint slick she out for money register while you trying to pressure her for digits to her cellular trying to get with her ya pockets are being measured up she faker then a mirage but you impressed with her cant sleep with her cause you slept on her she extra son whole body created myplayer but you obsessed with her yall both disrespect ya temple but now your checks done yall not letting God lead ya wanna have some fun but most times the outcome is her oven left with a bun while he run another baby mama strolling her young not choosing wisely might get caught again and have another one son alot of fake love only God teaches love thats whats up everybody chasing flesh walk with the spirit and trust its must but nah you in charge you your own boss yea I payed for mines you gonna pay for yours bad decisions really cost without God your lost so we dont listen we bugging we deserve nothing and live fronting we refuse to believe thats why we still struggling refuse to follow God then want to pass judgment we do our own thing in man we put our trust in we're all backwards only Christ is our comfort we gotta change soon the end will be sudden in the world is a battle mostly a sad one church hope you have one the bible better grab one repent today worship God or it could be your last one because the truth is that we are the bad ones.

These Attacks

Lord forgive me for my sins I repent once again this word is as much for me as it is as much for them and I want them to know in there mind spirit and soul that you are real and in control I'm just a servant playing my role we have to repent constantly and speak honestly passionately wait on the lord so we could see what he's got for our tree move with God make sure to tell em Jesus christ is the gate they need to believe and have faith because God's the only way.

So tough but keep striving living surviving attacks coming from all angles the Bermuda triangle stuck in the middle of hateration creating another trick to catch you another separation from family accusations more manipulation while you dodging temptation people starting to talk will you protect your reputation you fall but Christs keeps lifting you he's the truth got you in his hands and you will never lose lord regulate my every move need to know what should I choose theres more corruption more assumptions is he real is he fronting who's leaving Christ is coming only with there own click they running why is this so hard tell me why those saints didn't help me another fake handshake cause you aint got no fanbase some Christians out for themselves or they forgot to think straight tell me if you relate lets rock together not today we serving with our family another day lonely Jesus has to console me just another lesson learned watch out for other fonies only God get the glory backed into a corner not received in your own home the pain that you feel watching them disrespect Gods throne and this is not a game I will never disengage they persacute and perpetrate I'm screaming love not hate I speak the word with faith I have a new clean slate why dont you come my way God's your light to escape please dont turn away out the darkness and the Lord's got our back my armors is intact against all these attacks.

Brightside

Lord forgive me for my sins I repent once again this word is as much for me as it is as much for them and I want them to know in there mind spirit and soul that you are real and in control I'm just a servant playing my role we have to repent constantly and speak honestly passionately wait on the lord so we could see what he's got for our tree move with God make sure to tell em Jesus christ is the gate they need to believe and have faith because God's the only way.

We need you we are nothing without you please believe truth if you aint felt the holy spirit you still sleep dude if he aint touch you hush your mouth fellowships important now if you did you wouldn't doubt if you woke you'd worship his house and dont speak against it this blasphemy endless when church is done right the house of God is tremendous with blessings Joy and laughter while you praise em we all have to learning and growing faster without God you a disaster oh bless his holy name understanding pain understand the lies to keep em out your brain love and giving him all the glory its not our story its his story lord show me cause your the only one that truly knows me Jesus Christ shines his light unafraid steps you take at night lifted high you cant explain why but the Lord will be glorified I pray that you recognize to Christ give your life let him lead sacrifice like he did for us aaite love your brothers your mother and the others the lord will get you through God is remarkable thank you for your mercy we are not worthy to talk to you yet you still love us yet you still help us yet you still kept us without you we're breathless even though we lie your always on time put us back in line with only you in our mind then you show us will be alright plus you make us wise your the light aint no surprise that there's always brightside.

Abide in him

Lord forgive me for my sins I repent once again this word is as much for me as it is as much for them and I want them to know in there mind spirit and soul that you are real and in control I'm just a servant playing my role we have to repent constantly and speak honestly passionately wait on the lord so we could see what he's got for our tree move with God make sure to tell em Jesus christ is the gate they need to believe and have faith because God's the only way.

The answers you seek are found in our lord not in the street soe what you reap listen when God speaks learn when he teach we strong but we weak without God to lead we won't feed our tree put on the whole armor principalities get curbed with defeat the lord is to keep inside you everyday just to breath how else you gonna reach to preach when evil comes to compete its time to receive only God will make you complete never out of reach if you dont let your heart skip a beat stay centered with Christ hes life yes his love is divine he's the vine without him you cant intertwine or shine stay focused on the word and keep God on your mind living your life without guidance no assurance just violence without the lord look around you only trouble you finding ripping and grinding the devil playing you like a toy I'm here to make noise and only God can fill that viod full of dreadfulness aimlessness emptiness is dangerous the pursuit of happiness is only when God next to us with his special touch only one choice let him in he will abide in you and you must abide in him.

OTG one true God

Lord forgive me for my sins I repent once again this word is as much for me as it is as much for them and I want them to know in there mind spirit and soul that you are real and in control I'm just a servant playing my role we have to repent constantly and speak honestly passionately wait on the lord so we could see what he's got for our tree move with God make sure to tell em Jesus christ is the gate they need to believe and have faith because God's the only way.

Only him no propaganda no red candles or red Santa's no dead animals no statues no greedy bankers or gamblers no money no other person no idols should get by you worship Christ there's only one God should be beside you the 1 and only king of kings lord of lords prince of peace he's what you need aint no sacrifice like he did for you and me he got your best intrest but your only interested in things giving you gotta love God cause he's God and worship with true feelings believe his word when you reading apply what you receiving he's everything so not a thing could come before him leading no other spirits no Psychos or psychics Gods the one to call dont let holloween gass you up like a crystal ball can't play with Jesus you wont change my culture your fate is the fairy lake of burning sulfur keep christ in your heart forget the world do your part he's been here from the start got me out of the dark love him and praise em stay right there holy fire from the lord overhere if it ain't about christ I really dont care worship the one true God for life constantly theres only one make sure you follow the real O.T.G

Live for him

Lord forgive me for my sins I repent once again this word is as much for me as it is as much for them and I want them to know in there mind spirit and soul that you are real and in control I'm just a servant playing my role we have to repent constantly and speak honestly passionately wait on the lord so we could see what he's got for our tree move with God make sure to tell em Jesus christ is the gate they need to believe and have faith because God's the only way.

They like to say I'm just living life like everybody else having a good time but your on borrowed time a precious life that you wouldn't have without Christ but you disrespect him daily and you think your alright ask yourself did he not die for you did he not she'd blood in your place for your wickedness and sins and you still spit in his face everyday what you think after you know the truth there is nothing else no party no time no money no wealth could stop me chasing christ his words his life we can't live without him you do it cause your blind I pray that you could see I pray that you could hear 2 gifts he gave you and don't use em for him it's clear you could disappear you ain't gotta be here but you run yourself and think you know all be sincere I did it in the past I'm gifted built to last I'm lifted by my dad the Lord God brought me back and you should fear his wrath walking around gassed in the darkness living fast and everything material in the world turns to trash spiritual growth and gifts matter more Jesus Christ matters more try be holy cause he's holy only God could show you whats pure I'm sure you think your winning but you loosing your salvation be the creators creation and make him your dedication and heaven your destination promote God who's worth praising live for him God's amazing shout all glory to God through out the nation and stay patient while there hell raising stay close to his word my friend and always live for him.

God is perfect

Read the word of God so you could stay on the path follow his word best you can so you can last understand that no Temple's are perfect both ways so when your at church try not to be dismayed take the good leave the bad its all worth it they'll be surprises in the end because only God is perfect.

Queen goggles

I will marry you and confess my love before God and the whole world I will only have eyes for you yea you you go girl I will never hurt you your my partner your my queen we a team you are one of God's daughters the most beautifullest thing I've ever seen I will look at you with spiritual eyes know what I mean I need your help that's why I cry your my favorite dream I will help you because you give life I will guide you for eternity and lead you closer to Christ with his might I will pray with you and for you I will love you unconditionally and will never play you mentally or physically the holy spirit won't let me I'll respect your feelings I will have understanding in all situations I'm in love with your spirit so there's no hesitation we will praise the holy trinity and be 3 with God guiding us I will work hard and support you until the day your spirit is flying up I will uplift you and push you towards your goals and dreams trust and believe please these words I speak are everything I have experience in destroying relationships but God changed me now that God is in me I'll speak life while she gives life to a child straight from heaven Praise God and then my wife God's word is persice and me and her are just right I won't fail this time not with my new mind for Christ aaite !

All your money All your beauty All your anger All your stubbornness All your wrong teachings All your vanity All your hate All your Judgements All your selfishness All your racism will lead you to hell if you don't repent and surrender to the one true God who truly loves you and holds your Salvation.

its funny when I had drugs and liquor people will follow and listen to everything I say now I tell you God is real fam and none of us ain't going nowhere without him and it falls on death ears why because your blinded by this world so if reading this I rebuke the devil and all his works that is destroying your mind body and spirit and I pray that you have a strong encounter with our lord and Savior Jesus Christ so that you can understand that he is the way the truth and the life.

John 14:6

6 Jesus saith unto him, I am the way, the truth, and the life: no man cometh unto the Father, but by me.

Almost Everything in this world tears us apart except for those True Christian's full of light screaming in the dark I will not conform to this world and the Prince of the air I will keep my Faith in Jesus Christ who is always there we gotta chase God not money on the road to salvation all Glory to God Forever and ever its Christ Nation !!!

Light over Darkness

God's Time !!!

You chose or did God choose is he right or bad news was is it his looks height or money cause no Holy Spirit you lose you deserve no pain no hurt no lies you deserve true love you deserve no more cries just joy help and comfort right by your side the lord is our guide in him we rely till we die 3 cords tied for his Glory ya will shine no fornication before marriage stay forever on God's Time

Lord protect me

The endless battle we fight our flesh daily while encouraging others we suffer in pain and God always shows that he loves us I repent everyday and see myself growing we only here because his presence keeps us going thank you lord if not for spirit I'd be dead mentally physically spiritually covered in blood shed but the blood that you shed we didn't deserve your love is your word and your word forever is always confirmed lord please keep us close to you that's my concern I pray to stay in the light away from the darkness of this world.

Wisdom & Presence

Our wickedness got us here but God will free us a slave with no fear and God will clean us believers the seers the ones that enlighten such evil we fighting such lies we abiding the father of lies is conniving but with Yeshua I'm surviving inside I'm crying how they got us is sad I pray you know the whole truth and follow your dad our father up in heaven God is our only weapon his spirit gives us a message steering us through the reckless we need to stay in his presence.

No matter which way you go

you have nothing of yourselves only from where it grows will tell the importance of your spiritual health. Amen

All Glory to God !!!

Jesus only

Until this system is reconstructed it will always be corrupted no matter what sinner runs it if the holy spirit ain't upon him we still done wit run quick bow pray to one true God so he could clear up these lies and this facade people don't care about something that's not theres they just trying make money and others are running around scared I promise you I'm here this is

God's precious pearl who could lift it but him who will comfort the world only our lord in heaven get this message if you ain't exited for the lake of fire receive his presence in the name of the father the son and the Holy Spirit our only weapon we good over here fam I ain't threatened my light bright all day only Jesus I'ma mention God is never phony keep the faith you won't be lonely you already know who told me I walk with Jesus only.

The Air up there

Flying through the air without a care living however you want do you know who put you there do you even care where you from I pray you do indeed you make others believe but keep them grounded because only you is what they see you living it up so close to the sky but you not pointing up your take off is a breath of fresh air fans everywhere got the flare to go higher trying to reach the top and pass number 1 unsatisfied with your space you continue to jump oh yeah it feels great cause you walking on air but today idol worship is a virus called corona so prepare still at your best still not giving respect still flying until you start having shortness of breath could it be the very thing you mastered is going to leave your respiratory different no more flying just fatigue feeling weak can't compete hard to breathe hard to speak God gave you life he's everything you need now it's to late down to your last breath God blew breath into your lungs where's his respect God giveth and take away don't take life for granted today he made you you was born for his Glory to celebrate.

God is more important then me If you like me or my music or anything of me I want you to know it's all God my life and everything in it must be for his Glory if I can't point to God I'm nothing and I don't know him so I want you to follow him not me focus on God please focus on God !!!

To My true Father in heaven thank you Lord may God bless us all and give strength to all Families to the Father's we lost kids won't be able to see them today and I'm torn we need change I pray for change my lord.

(Veelito All Glory to God)

Everyday

Every day blind ones are dying every day lost one's are finding our Savior healing and supplying Every day people are crying weather its desperation and pain or joyful tears when we claim that we are nothing without God and that he is everything we need to repent Everyday is heaven sent Everyday its God's Glory we need God not men Every day I Praise his name my Praise from him it came understand that God is first then my talents and anything Every day I breath the air he gave he's the one who makes me brave fighting the good fight against the evil that we made God is in control God is real he who has a ear hear it I Pray that all those chosen be blessed by Holy Spirit.

Amen !!!

The Lie is over

The lie is over Yahshuah skin of bronze hair of wooly the deception will go no further from these bullies the lie is over we are the truly God's people we started with God and we will overcome evil and God will finish what God started in us guided by the Holy Spirit we conquerors driven we living everlasting through Christ Jesus this is fact we leaders and all demons devils ain't never gonna beat us God will fight for us that's christ in us and light defeats darkness with righteousness yea rock with this its truth so we gotta go hard Yahshuah forever all Glory to God.

Light over darkness story

[ ] I was supposed to record a video to a song called another day another dollar in Miami but it didn't happen and then I was supposed to come back to the X to do the second video in the hood with a second single called Off this lol this was the last worldly track I did that didn't happen either God changed me what else is new I sold drugs practically my whole life and this last time we was moving drugs and somebody close to me went to jail this is the way it happened on my birthday was I was usually with him like always on the pickup moving keys of dope and the day before my birthday it was time for me to go but this time I couldn't I wanted to be there so bad but couldn't flights was cancelled busses already left God didn't want me to go he wanted to show me his mercy and his word the crazy thing is a week before my mother and sister was telling me that they was praying for me and that God was gonna save me and take me out the street life I wasn't trying to hear that honestly thought it was nonsense but it stuck in my mind so on my birthday while someone went to jail God took the blinders off of me and then God sent someone to tell me it was him and show me what church to go to all on my birthday God is real and God is amazing.

[ ] Just cause you felt the Holy spirit and God has changed you doesn't mean your free from error you have to let him lead you have to hang on to Jesus Christ hang on to the light and stay away from the darkness days after I got baptized I went to church on a Sunday I was playing sports and I was late to church so I didn't change clothes but that day God's glory fell on the whole church and on me too I was granted repentance and I was crying screaming holding on to a chair and was filled with the Holy spirit God is a hundred percent real and I'm terribly sorry for you if you can't feel him or don't believe Because God is awesome I constantly tell people don't let the devil lie to you because for years he lied to me so hold your bible tight light over Darkness stand firm I was lost thought I was winning but I was losing using drugs and selling stealing lying doing evil things on the brink of death or jail funny it never happened God had another plan I felt I was tough and now that I know God is real I'm nothing without him

[ ] I was in a situation after where I was lied to by a so called friend who conned me said he was gonna help me but it ended up being a bank scam and I was left holding the bag because it was in my name while others got away with thousands and I ended up in jail and got probation but God used me in prison I prayed for others I thought I wouldn't see my kids ever but I was also taught a lesson not to do things without God I jumped into something I didn't even pray on it but God got me out I was in a dark place now I'm free and I walk in the light but to walk in Da light you gotta find Jesus Christ I pray your chosen God was with me like always till I was released

Stand firm I tell people if you gangster fight your flesh real gangsters wake up in the morning and pray real gangsters live there life for Christ all day real gangsters fight there flesh and say amen real gangsters follow God real gangsters are the apostles who died for Christ just like I made errors as a Christian and still I have to fight my flesh daily we all do. Not one of us is good only God is holy we got a long way to go were all bad ones thinking that we're good no one's good nah so live for God stay in the word I eat it and spit it lift his name put him high lift the lord up I'm a messenger God up the bible is the living word God is the truth the way and the life let me talk to em with the word there's a lot of fake prophet's anti-Christ people those that may know the word but are evil are the worst you could know the word and not have the Holy spirit there's a lot of wickedness in this world so be not lovers of the world by their fruit you will know them stay close to God pray and fast let him lead it's the only way you'll survive we all need God daily we have turned or back on him and God gave me my talents and everything he's giving me is for his Glory please understand what comes out my mouth is from God not me the world is constantly programming evil be not of the world God bless you all I pray for change you ain't gotta be what they say God is way let the healing begin I pray for change light over Darkness God's the truth time to break the cycle the lord will make you brand new I pray for change Pray God chooses you yes indeed let the holy spirit lead it's time for you to believe I pray for change only God can satisfy your living he's the vine better listen God will make you shine different I'm gonna shine for the loooord what he gives they can't take away hmm I'm going to shine for the lord let thy will be done in meeee God bless you all.

Different Praises story

Going through a pandemic people in fear people out of work church is closed feeling stuck but I will still Praise you lord I will still Pray daily I will still worship you and you only there's a lot of misguided individuals there's a lot of false preaching false religions worship of other God's Lord I pray for them that are lost there's only one God and I will forever Praise him please worship God alone swiftly after an injustice that's been going on for years has spiked completely out of control the community erupted the pain has destroyed millions of people the message sent to our youth is the worst thing I fear. The words black lives matter not the movement the words is a truth in injustice against racism against oppression to all minorities against inequality we have seen this for years of course all lives matter of course God only matters above all but this moment was about police brutality and racism against us and the loss of our brothers and sisters the word says in romans 14:11 For it is written: " As I live, says the LORD, Every knee shall bow to Me, And every tongue shall confess to God."

so I say every knee shall bow let's praise the lord together right now because God has no colorlines God is the answer God can change anyone our lord and Savior teaches us to love one another not hate but a lot of this was planned there's evil in the world there's evil forces that buy people silence there's evil people that worship money above all things there's a group of sellouts that help manipulate the masses with evildoers and I won't be bought I know God is 100 percent real he's inside of a lot people I see him all in my vision he walks with me so comfortably what you believe come talk to me what I don't care God over everything money money, money the root of all evil this place says its foundation is God but it's not we took God out schools we took God out of everything the money says in God we trust but that's not our God we need to bring back God in everything we need God America this place the blind leading the blind God help us then I saw how our young woman were being destroyed baby mothers everywhere kids with no fathers woman being dominated by money living in fornication and their daughters following them in an endless generational curses men with men and woman with women and women attracted to the wrong man for all the wrong reasons man that that supposed to lead our woman closer to God take advantage and destroy them woman becoming one flesh with 30 guys polluting themselves with many different spirits God doesn't want this I rebuke the devil and all his works wake up girl your blinded you go for the physical when you should let God lead you spiritually. And then at the end of all this finally I feel pressure I feel hurt I feel drained I feel like I can't go on I'm tired of falling myself I'm tired of my weak flesh I want it to burn away forever so that my spirit can go with God.

Purpose talk

Stop complaining about what you went through and start celebrating what you got through with God!!!
He will never leave you don't get caught by religious spirits what God started he will finish.
Chosen before the worlds foundation chosen for his Glory and salvation.

The picture is big with us
and with God we will go far we
can't turn back or look
away we will fall like Peter
if we stall our faith
in God must be above all
we must trust his plan
and we must stand tall.

Veelito

Nobody cares until it's the end
Nobody cares until
it happens to them
Nobody cares
that world is trying to control ya
Nobody cares but I bet someone told ya
no one believes until evil
takes over
Nobody cares
Just God and his soldiers

Veelito

God is love, Love comes from
God and God is forever
And love conquers all !!!

♥

Always put God first
God's word and his laws are
More important then your feelings.

(leap of faith)
Walking with God we will
succeed I promise to cherish
what he gives to me he will
lead and we will follow I see
paradise in his eyes and a
better tommorow one flesh
one life and or savior Jesus
Christ will keep us safe I love
you our love is a step away
just a leap of faith!!!

- Veelito

(God's work)
I will not throw in the towel
I will Die with my boots
on I will for Gods will.

Veelito

We are broken and empty without God we won't survive the Holy spirit is our light and our Guide !!!

The more you love the more I love the more God's glory shines from above because we love we will stay strong God is love in him we trust God's for you God's for us.

- veelito

WITHOUT CHRIST WE ARE LOST IN
DEATH GOD IS LOVE AND LIFE THE ONE
TRUE PROPHET AT HIS BEST THE WORLD
IS FULL OF LIES SUCH DARKNESS SUCH
A MESS ASK YOURSELF WHAT WILL YOUR
SOUL SAY TO GOD WHEN YOU LOSE ALL
YOUR FLESH.

Veelito

We are all sinners especially
me aint no excuse the least I
can do is tell you the truth
God's 100 percent real you
need to wake up my friend
there's no us without Christ
there's no me without him !!!

Veelito

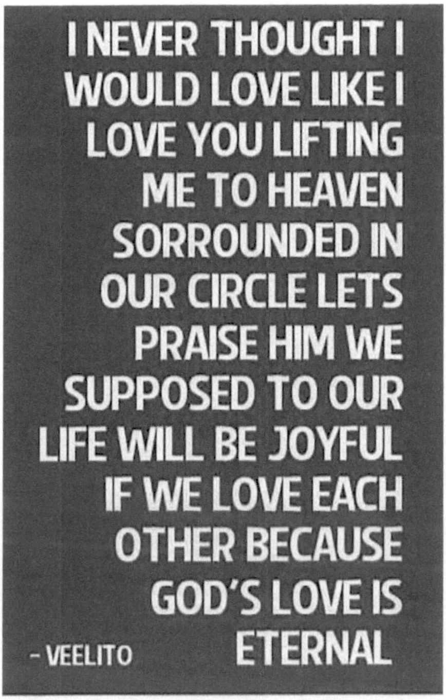

I NEVER THOUGHT I WOULD LOVE LIKE I LOVE YOU LIFTING ME TO HEAVEN SORROUNDED IN OUR CIRCLE LETS PRAISE HIM WE SUPPOSED TO OUR LIFE WILL BE JOYFUL IF WE LOVE EACH OTHER BECAUSE GOD'S LOVE IS ETERNAL
- VEELITO
QuotePixel.com

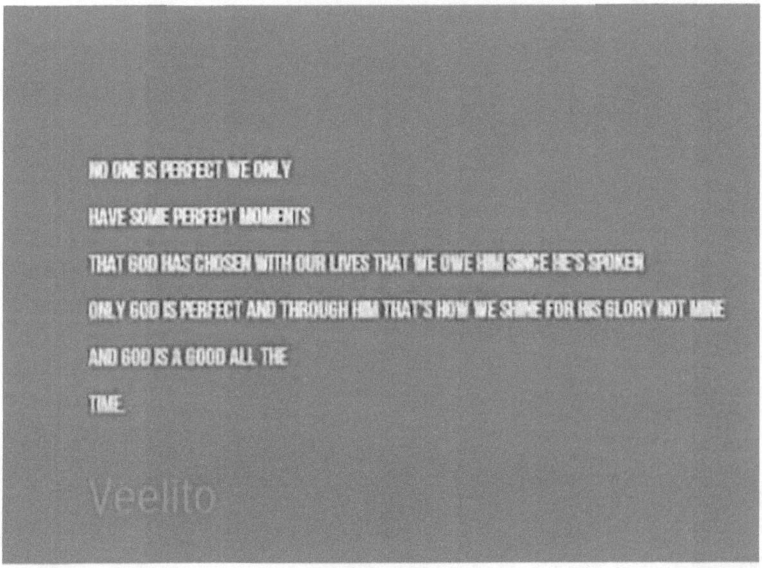

NO ONE IS PERFECT WE ONLY
HAVE SOME PERFECT MOMENTS
THAT GOD HAS CHOSEN WITH OUR LIVES THAT WE OWE HIM SINCE HE'S SPOKEN
ONLY GOD IS PERFECT AND THROUGH HIM THAT'S HOW WE SHINE FOR HIS GLORY NOT MINE
AND GOD IS A GOOD ALL THE
TIME.
Veelito

(Poetry)

poem called

(God's children)

Some call me a mistake a
error a problem a terror but
I'm a blessing from God and
it dont get no better see I'm
from him and I'm part of you
it's not my fault till this day
that I'm being made even if
you don't want me true but
your the mother how could
you move this way so
selfishly that's innocent baby
killing me is crazy thou shall
not commit murder even if
you angry lady you suppose
to be my safety the one that
feeds me daily so I'm here I'm
moving I'm growing I'm
kicking and you just gonna
make a decision that you
don't want me living you
kidding first they rip off my
leg then they rip off arm and
then they squeeze my head
pull me out and I'm gone I
hope your a proud mom for
sure round of applause you
just killed an innocent baby
that truly wasn't yours I pray
ya'll forgiven by God.

- Veelito

Lord today I Pray for those
long lost soldiers today I Pray
that those chosen will
recognize today what God
has done for them and will
understand that God has
created them for his Glory
that they have to live for God
and praise and worship his
name in the continuance of
spreading of the Gospel to all.
If you have faith I'm speaking
to you God has chosen you
for his Glory thank you lord
for all that you have done
and continue to do we are
nothing without God and no
matter what goes on God is
more important then
everything so please
understand that by the will of
God we have been granted
grace chosen before the
foundation of the world that
we should be holy and
without blame before him in
love. Having predestined us
to adoption as sons by Jesus
Christ himself according to
the good pleasure of his will.
Today I pray for the lost
today we will stand with our
savior from now till forever
we will fight the good fight
with the strength of our God
and give him all the Glory
Forever in the name of the
Father the Son and the Holy
spirit Amen !!!

(Veelito) All Glory to God

(Amazing love)

Just amazing God's love
beyond words to say I'm
touched forever everyday
I'm moved in everyway
when you teach I feel
tears of joy inside of me
then I dream of you this
love is so pure yes I
believe there's much to
do forever I know love
will succeed I trust in our
lord your right next to
me I constantly need
your presence if not I
can't breath I feel it
cause we're close I feel it
when I read and most of
the time in my temple I
know everything is right
when I catch a glimpse of
love working so pure full
of light this is all for
God's glory thank you
lord Jesus Christ I'm
blessed to know this
amazing love the love of
my life.

- Veelito

126

How could you say he loves you if he's making you live in
fornication disrespecting God daily if a man doesn't have
God he doesn't have true love so how could he love you ask
yourself a question if couldn't have sex with you would he be
with you listen the best reason to be in love is because you
both love God without Jesus christ there is no love because
God is love.

- Veelito

The calmness around you I
need you to survive
You give me strength to rise
your vision is mines touching
so many lives our hearts can't
deny
I love you so much our
connection won't die I can't
turn back now that's no lie
forgive me please I love you
to me it was a surprise now i
see the glory of God so I cry
thank you christ your always
on time.

- Veelito

(Purpose talk)
Believe in God's Promises
Worship God only
Love your brothers
Let His Spirit Lead
Fast & Pray
Be the word of God

All Glory to God Forever
We are nothing without God !!!
We deserve nothing !!!
But he still loves us !!!
Worship him only !!!
Praise Him !!!
Live your life for Christ !!!
let him Lead !!!
Only God can satisfy you !!!
Light Over Darkness !!!
God over Everything !!!

FINAL THOUGHTS

I just want to say that God is 100 percent real and I'm blessed to be alive from where I came from and after everything that I have been through my mind is different because of God and I'm now striving to make a difference in the world bringing light not darkness bringing hope and peace and righteousness speaking life through poetry through music through clothing through basketball forever promoting our lord and savior Jesus Christ and I pray that those who read me see me or hear me have an encounter with God in the name of the Father the Son and the Holy Spirit AMEN !!!